REKINDLE THE GIFT OF GOD

ROCH KERESZTY, O.CIST.

Rekindle the Gift of God

A Handbook for Priestly Life

IGNATIUS PRESS   SAN FRANCISCO

Cover art:
Tabernacle door (detail)
Billy Hassel
Our Lady of Dallas Abbey, Irving, Texas

Cover design by Enrique J. Aguilar

© 2021 by Ignatius Press, San Francisco
All rights reserved
ISBN 978-1-62164-405-7 (PB)
ISBN 978-1-64229-162-9 (eBook)
Library of Congress Control Number 2020946602
Printed in the United States of America ∞

CONTENTS

PREFACE

The twelfth century is commonly thought to have been a time of flourishing Christian faith and culture. Saint Bernard, however, sums up the state of the Church with this verse from Isaiah: "From the sole of the foot even to the head, there is no soundness in it" (Is 1:6). He chastises the greed of the clergy and the sale of ecclesiastical offices, as well as the heterosexual and homosexual sins of supposedly celibate priests and bishops. Yet he also acknowledges that there is a powerful reform movement growing in the Church: exemplary Cistercian and Benedictine monks are being chosen for bishops, and eventually a Cistercian, Blessed Eugene III, is elected to the See of Saint Peter.

Our own day also shows many positive signs of renewal. We see the growth of sound religious orders in the Church, the formation of new lay and religious communities (although many old ones disappear), and the martyrdoms of many, both young and old, who would sooner die than deny their faith. They are from all over the world—the Middle East, Africa, and India—and they far outnumber the martyrs of the ancient Roman Empire.

Yet, the same judgment of Isaiah aptly describes the current mood of many Catholics in the West. Even though the great majority of the clergy have been involved neither in the sexual abuse of minors nor in other sexual sins, and the majority of bishops have not knowingly condoned abuse, great crimes and terribly grave omissions have nonetheless been committed by a significant minority. Now the entire

Church appears, in the eyes of the world, treacherous and corrupted. Bishop Robert Barron identifies the diabolic dimension of the crisis:

> I challenge anyone to come up with a more devastatingly effective strategy for attacking the mystical body of Christ than the abuse of children and young people by priests. This sin had countless direct victims of course, but it also crippled the Church financially, undercut vocations, caused people to lose confidence in Christianity, dramatically compromised attempts at evangelization, etc., etc. It was a diabolical masterpiece.[1]

Of course, Barron adds, without the cooperation of weak and wicked members of the clergy, the Devil could not have carried out his plan. As Pope Francis suggested in one of his impromptu homilies, if in any age the Church does not cleanse herself, God allows the Devil to do the cleaning in his own way. He uncovers her hidden sins, makes a mockery of her teachings, and destroys the credibility of her leaders. Usually, the immediate result is a helpless rage and confusion in the ranks of the faithful majority. But just as at the end of the Roman Empire—a time of barbarian invasions and corrupt popes and clergy—the healthy members and leaders of the Church, God-sent saints and fervent communities, began cleaning up the festering wounds, and Pope Francis is promoting a new missionary impetus.

Today, the renewal takes place on many different levels and in various ways. We need a well-formed, active laity to be a healthy counterbalance for keeping the clergy true to its own vocation, but we also need a renewed clergy. In

[1] Robert Barron, "The McCarrick Mess", *Word on Fire*, August 9, 2018, https://www.wordonfire.org/resources/article/the-mccarrick-mess/5873/.

fact, a new generation of seminarians and priests is already beginning to emerge—many call them the "JPII generation": they are happy in their priesthood and convinced of the greatness of their vocation. The best ones are not infected with the persistent virus of clericalism. They do not look down on their parishioners but inspire them with reverence and love to be their co-workers in building up the community. They refuse to be squeezed into the straitjacket of yesterday's definitions of the priestly role. They do not want to be mere "sacramental ministers" or "community organizers". The choice between "celebrating the sacraments" or "celebrating life" appears to them a meaningless dichotomy: they know that the former is inseparable from the latter. Their ideal is to become like Paul, a servant of Jesus Christ. Aware of their inadequacy, they still accept the responsibility of representing Christ. They mediate to their people His sanctifying words and actions; in fact, they make Christ Himself present for them in the sacrifice of the Eucharist. Thus, these priests plan to shape and form their people into the one Body of Christ so that they may offer themselves as a "living sacrifice for the glory of the Father". If a priest is successful in this work, the Eucharist will naturally transform the life of his community. Then those who truly recognize Christ in the Eucharist will also recognize Him in their suffering neighbors. The charity flowing from the Eucharist will mobilize the laity to reach out beyond the narrow confines of their parish. When outsiders observe their gatherings, they will be as stunned as the second-century pagans: "Look ... how they love one another!"[2] Such communities

---

[2] Tertullian, *Apology*, ch. 39, in *Tertullian and Minucius Felix*, trans. T.R. Glover, Loeb Classical Library 250 (Cambridge, Mass.: Harvard University Press, 1931).

become magnets in our world, where growing crowds of loners are separated from one another despite the ever more sophisticated means of mass communication.

The new priest then, to quote Vatican II, will be both a friend and a father for his parishioners. In fact, a good priest, according to Saint Paul and Saint Bernard, is also a loving mother for his people. He is their father who begets them by the word of the Gospel as well as their mother who is in birth pangs until Christ is formed in them (1 Cor 4:15; Gal 4:19).

ACKNOWLEDGMENTS

I am very grateful to Jean-Paul Juge for editing the manuscript and to the Ignatius Press production department, who not only completed the editing process but with great empathy enriched and fine-tuned the content of the work.

INTRODUCTION

The post–Vatican II Church rediscovered a half-forgotten biblical truth: God calls every baptized Christian to holiness. This holiness does not consist of extraordinary mortifications. Rather, it is the perfection of love, the attainment of which is made possible by God's offer of His Holy Spirit to each one of us. As a result, each Christian receives from God a unique gift by which he is to build up the community of the Church. All this served to correct a one-sided preconciliar perspective: before the Council, the average Catholic often saw religious life and the priesthood as *the* way to holiness and service for the Church.

Today, however, the pendulum has swung to the opposite extreme: most Catholics in the United States no longer perceive religious life or the priesthood as a challenge addressed to them. Yet while the number of practicing Catholics shrank considerably in the postconciliar decades, the generosity and religious zeal of many American Catholics has in fact increased after the Council. There are more lay people than ever before who choose to work for the Church even though they could have a more financially successful career elsewhere. I also believe that God's inner call to the priesthood and religious life is just as present now as ever before. However, supporting persons and structures are scarce today. Few parents encourage and assist their growing children in discerning a vocation; few priests and religious reflect to young people an inner certainty of their own vocation's value.

Yet wherever bishops and priests personally nurture vocations, seminaries fill up once again.

This new handbook is intended to be what used to be called a *vade mecum* ("go with me" in Latin), a companion for the priest in his formation, ministry, and life. It contains the essentials regarding the discernment of vocations, the mystery of the Catholic priesthood, the basic priestly virtues, preaching, the preparation of the faithful for the sacraments (especially reconciliation and marriage), and the most frequent problems encountered with different age groups and kinds of people. At the end, it outlines the basics of spiritual direction or guidance.

In writing this book, I relied on my own experience of fifty-nine years in priestly ministry, on the experiences of my fellow priests, and on the Cistercian tradition. I hope and pray that this short handbook will be a help to those discerning vocations and will serve many priests, young and old, in rethinking, deepening, and renewing their priestly ideal and praxis.

CHAPTER 1

Discerning a Vocation

God addresses us in an endless variety of ways, and each one of us perceives God's voice through the mediation of his own personality. We cannot find two exactly identical vocation stories. Still, there are some general patterns found in almost all vocation stories, and we can recognize an assortment of signs that often indicate the first stages of a vocation. Though every person receives a personal call from God, I will limit myself here to describing the genesis of a priestly or religious vocation.

SIGNS OF A VOCATION

In every vocation, two factors are at play, at times in tandem but often in conflict. One is the human heart; the other—infinitely greater than the heart but present in its deepest recesses—is the call of God. In an obedient and sensitive soul, God's call penetrates and activates the deepest longings of the heart, and the soul soon intuits or at least suspects that his own deepest desires manifest God's call. In other cases, the call reaches a distracted, inattentive, or hardened heart that does not notice what is happening or even refuses outright to respond to the call. In such cases, the call is perceived as a burden, a confusing and disquieting obstacle to freedom and happiness. But when the soul decides to obey it, peace and joy are gradually restored, and the soul begins to desire God's will. This is the beginning of real prayer, as we will see in chapter 3.

Yet, as a wise old priest remarked, it is possible to abort a vocation. The soul's long resistance or voluntary hearing loss may have built up such a thick wall that God's gentle voice cannot reach the depths of the heart. The hardened soul, however, must pay a price for his resistance: as long as he closes off his deepest self to God, he also prevents himself from living out of his own depth. Such a soul must live—so to speak—on the surface, out of touch with his own deepest self where God waits for him.[1] In what follows, I would like to sketch out some telltale signs that may indicate an authentic vocation.

1. Dissatisfaction

One of the initial signs of God's call may be a deep dissatisfaction with what one has and what one is now. This is very different from self-hatred or hatred of the world. Rather, it comes from an awareness that all the possible careers one could pursue, all the possessions he could accumulate, and even his best friendships could never be enough. A person in this state is not insensitive to joy. On the contrary, enjoying a landscape or a piece of art or literature or talking to a friend begets in him a longing that none of these experiences can satisfy. C. S. Lewis describes one form of this yearning:

---

[1] Obviously, this does not mean that such a soul will end up in hell. In fact, a late wake-up call may inspire in the person who refused the initial grace a resolute striving to make up for the missed vocation through a selfless, service-oriented life.

As I stood beside a flowering currant bush on a summer day there suddenly arose in me without warning, and as if from a depth not of years but of centuries, the memory of that earlier morning at the Old House when my brother had brought his toy garden into the nursery. It is difficult to find words strong enough for the sensation which came over me; Milton's "enormous bliss of Eden" (giving the full, ancient meaning to "enormous") comes somewhere near it. It was a sensation, of course, of desire; but desire for what? ... Before I knew what I desired, the desire itself was gone, the whole glimpse withdrawn, the world turned commonplace again.[2]

At times we too may remember "the enormous bliss of Eden", the intimations of infinite joy, love, and goodness, as we yearn to reach that Reality for which our present life provides only a foretaste.

2. Gratitude

Someone else may start from an experience that at first seems very much opposed to dissatisfaction and longing—gratitude. But once it unfolds, it will appear as another aspect of C. S. Lewis' experience. You may find an intense joy in living and discover in all that surrounds you—say, a morning sunrise or a good conversation—signs and messages of Someone. Everything and everyone around you, all that happens to you, becomes a personal gift that fills you with gratitude. In Fyodor Dostoyevsky's novel *The Brothers Karamazov*, a young man who will later become Father Zossima sees this overflowing joy and thankfulness in his brother who is dying from tuberculosis. This experience marks the beginning of his monastic vocation:

[2] C. S. Lewis, *Surprised by Joy: The Shape of My Early Life* (San Diego: Harcourt Brace & Company, 1955), p. 16.

"Well, doctor, have I another day in this world?" he would ask, joking.

"You'll live many days yet," the doctor would answer, "and months and years too."

"Months and years!" he would exclaim. "Why reckon the days? One day is enough for a man to know all happiness. My dear ones, why do we quarrel, try to outshine each other and keep grudges against each other? Let's go straight into the garden, walk and play there, love, appreciate, and kiss each other, and glorify life". . . .

The windows of his room looked into a garden, and our garden was a shady one, with old trees in it which were coming into bud. The first birds of spring were flitting in the branches, chirruping and singing at the windows. And looking at them and admiring them, he began suddenly begging their forgiveness too: "Birds of heaven, happy birds, forgive me, for I have sinned against you too." None of us could understand that at the time, but he shed tears of joy. "Yes," he said, "there was such glory of God all about me: birds, trees, meadows, sky: only I lived in shame and dishonored it all and did not notice the beauty and glory."[3]

Having seen the beauty and glory of God in His creatures, one may begin to desire the source of all beauty and glory. And in particular, if he has experienced how good, pure, and noble a human being can be, he may begin to yearn for the source of all purity, nobility, and goodness. In a mood of overflowing gratitude, he wants to dedicate his life to Him in a direct and radical way. He cannot imagine for himself any other way of life than living in His presence and serving Him in everything.

[3] *The Brothers Karamazov*, trans. Constance Garnett (New York: The Modern Library, 1996), pp. 321–22.

3. An Encounter with Jesus Christ

Another vocation may arise from getting acquainted with the person of Jesus Christ. In reading the Scriptures or talking to a holy Christian, he encounters the One Who calls him: "Come and follow me." He may at first wish he did not hear Him. He then tries to go about his business as if nothing happened. But he cannot. He becomes aware that he no longer belongs to himself. He cannot, in good conscience, arrange his future as he wishes. Christ wants him to give up everything and follow Him. At those times when he feels inclined to obey Him, an immense peace overtakes him; when he decides to refuse Him, he becomes sad and escapes into distractions.

4. The Desire to Help People

For some people, a vocation may start with a strong desire to help people. Someone asks himself, "How could I help people in the best way possible?" He dreams about becoming a doctor, a psychiatrist, a social worker, a teacher, or a nurse, but one day he discovers that giving Christ to people matters more than anything else. Uniting them to the Body of Christ in the Eucharist, giving them His peace in the Sacrament of Penance, shaping and forming Christ in them through teaching and prayer—this is what appeals to him most. Healing their souls and bodies for eternal life appears to him more important than curing them temporarily from bodily or psychological disease.

Close to this type is that of the "community builder". This sort of person knows he has a natural ability to create good community spirit. People instinctively turn to him for leadership. They sense his security and feel at home in his presence. His enthusiasm is contagious; he can reconcile antagonists and inspire common projects. Christ may call such a natural leader into His service. In that case, the called one will have to build not just any community, but the "Body of Christ", the gathering of those in whom Christ Himself provides a home for the estranged and lonely people of today's world.

5. Love of the Liturgy

We find many people who are attracted to the religious life and to the priesthood because they are in love with the liturgy. This love may be the sign of an authentic vocation. After all, the central act of the ministerial priesthood from which everything else derives and to which everything else leads is the celebration of the Eucharist. For every religious, too, the center of the day is the Eucharist. If someone seeks *the spiritual reality* that the rite expresses, if he is moved by the love of Christ Who gives Himself to the Father and to the Church in the Eucharist, his vocation will develop in the right direction. But it is not enough to appreciate *only* the experience of beauty in the liturgy or to seek *only* the warmth and shelter of a human community. Still worse, some seek the altar in order to cover up a deep-seated feeling of inferiority; they want to bask in the aura of borrowed holiness and pontificate over the faithful through the power of the ritual and of preaching. These are clear signs that such a person has no vocation at all or has distorted a beginning vocation.

THE NATURAL DRIVING FORCES OF A VOCATION

Everyone who responds to God's call must draw on some natural "energy resource". Without harnessing a natural driving force, no vocation could survive in the long run.

It would collapse into a psychological vacuum. The Lord builds upon nature.

1. Ambition

For instance, the ambition to do something really important, to become someone who "counts", may be a precious resource that God's grace can use and transform. At the beginning, a person longs to become important in the eyes of his parents, in the eyes of his social milieu, or at least in his own eyes. But if he listens to Christ, he will learn to lose his life in order to gain it. He will also learn to please God more than he pleases men and to accept the indifference and even the rejection of people for God's sake. He may thereby trust God so much that he can put both himself and his work into God's hands and no longer fear appearing empty-handed before his Creator.

2. Leadership

Likewise, someone with leadership potential will learn to become a good leader. Instead of pushing people around as a domineering tyrant, he will learn to support, inspire, and coordinate the talents of everyone for a common purpose. When encountering opposition, envy, or hatred, and when discovering his own unpurified motives, he will learn humility and patience. He will realize how little he can do by himself. God alone builds the house and produces the harvest. The servant must do his best but ultimately attribute the results to the One from Whom all good comes.

3. Intellectual Interests

Intellectual curiosity may also be very useful for God's work. Not only theology, but any study of the world and of man is, in the final analysis, a study of God's truth and therefore sacred. If an intellectual devotes himself to God's service, he will become a better intellectual. Instead of being a complacent possessor and condescending dispenser of the treasures of knowledge, he will remain a student all his life. Aware of his limitations, he will always be drawn to learn more. Whatever aspect of the world is his field of inquiry and teaching, his respect and desire for the truth will inspire in his audience a respect and desire for God.

Let me illustrate this with a true story. During the Communist era, the thinker and choreographer Valéria Dienes was interviewed on the state-controlled Hungarian television network. She was already in her nineties, but still in full possession of her extraordinary intellectual powers that made her an internationally known philosopher and linguist. She also had a deep Christian faith that transformed and inspired her scholarly research. The interviewer carefully avoided any religious topic. Yet, after the TV show, Dienes received a letter. "I had never heard about you before, for I am just a boiler smith", the correspondent explained, "but while listening to you, I came to realize that God must exist." This is the apostolate of an intellectual. Without even speaking about God, she could not help radiating a reverence and love for truth that pointed beyond herself to the Source of all truth.

4. Aesthetic Sensitivity

The aesthetically inclined individual also has much to offer to God. Sensitivity to beauty may develop into sensitivity to God. He can also use his aesthetic talents to develop a beautiful liturgy and beautiful surroundings for the liturgy. But he also must undergo a conversion, a reevaluation of his values. Truth, honesty, simplicity, and love must be placed before and above any aesthetic value. Paradoxically, if the aesthete prefers honesty, humility, and truth to cultivating beauty, even his aesthetic taste will develop; he will come to understand that beauty and truth are inseparable.

CHARACTERISTICS COMMON TO ALL VOCATIONS

Regardless of the variety of forms that religious and priestly vocations may take, we can identify three common characteristics in each of them: passion for God, ability to love people, and readiness to learn from criticism.

1. Passion for God

Many of the signs and driving forces of vocations that I mentioned earlier may also be found in people who are not called to be priests or religious. What points to a particular vocation to the priesthood or religious life is the singular intensity of passion that manifests itself in various forms: in yearning for something greater than this world can give, in gratitude to God, in readiness to serve Christ and people. In other words, a good vocation always has the potential to develop a passionate "adventure of love" with God. It happens in many different ways, but it is always the same basic experience: the one called knows that there is no greater joy than loving God and serving Him directly. Marrying and giving life to children may be a beautiful way to God for other people, but for him, it would be a compromise. In comparison to his Beloved, nothing else counts. Such a soul will appreciate the prayer of Saint Francis—"My God and my all"—or Saint Thomas Aquinas' answer to Christ when He offered him anything he wanted: "Only you, Lord." We cannot expect this love to be aflame at the very beginning, but the soul must have *the desire* to love God and be ready to pay any price for learning to do it.

2. Capacity to Love People

In Christianity, the love of God and the love of neighbor are inseparable. A document of the Cistercian General Chapter has put it with classic precision: "Our love should, in a single, undivided act, embrace God and neighbor, our neighbor who has been created in the image of God and redeemed by the blood of Christ. Therefore true love should manifest itself in the twofold service of God and man."[4] This applies not only to an active apostolic life, but also to those in exclusively contemplative communities. We can easily delude ourselves about where we stand with God. We may enjoy a sweet, heartfelt peace and think that we are in love with God; but if we do not care about the people around us, we are deceiving ourselves. A genuine vocation always includes the desire and the ability to love others for their own sakes rather than as objects of our good works. If someone is incapable of honesty in personal relationships and is merely playing a role, if he cannot sincerely give and receive, then religious life or the priesthood would only aggravate his problem. But if you feel that you cannot love, even though you have the desire to love, there is no reason to despair. God is ready to do miracles for one who has faith the size of a mustard seed. "Ask and it will be given you; seek, and you shall find; knock and it will be opened to you. For every one who asks receives, and he who seeks finds, and to him

---

[4] "Cistercian Life Today: Declaration of the General Chapter of the Cistercian Order", no. 42, in *Pathways to Charity* (printed by the Our Lady of Dallas Cistercian Abbey, 2005), p. 41.

who knocks it will be opened" (Lk 11: 9–10). God can heal even the most timid person who has withdrawn from others for fear of rejection. He can make us overcome our dread of loving and being loved.

3. Readiness to Learn from Criticism

The most dangerous trap on our way to God is our unlimited potential for rationalization. I can easily convince myself that I am kind, generous, and loving while everybody around me clearly sees that I am obnoxious and condescending. At the same time, I am surprised when my friend does not see how irritating his self-righteous tone of voice can be. Others often see and judge our actions more objectively than we do. This is one of the reasons why priestly formation and religious life require living in community. I cannot know myself, let alone improve my relationship with God and with others, unless I am positively eager to receive criticism. The balloon of self-importance needs to be pierced and deflated so that I can learn and accept truth about myself. At the beginning, this is a very bitter truth and almost impossible to swallow. I feel I am a hopeless case; I am unable to love God and people sincerely. But hitting rock bottom is at the same time a moment of grace: I no longer put myself—not even unconsciously—above others, but begin to accept them as fellow sinners. I understand that my neighbors and I, all of us *together*, need God's forgiveness. Thus, accepting the truth about myself is the road to accepting others and adopting the right relationship with God. One must beg for mercy rather than expect a reward.

However, it is not enough to wait passively for God's forgiveness. While waiting for His grace to transform my heart, I must work on myself with all my strength. As a maxim attributed to Saint Ignatius of Loyola puts it, "It is wrong to measure a man's progress by his facial expressions, gestures, good nature, or love of solitude. Instead, it should be measured by the discipline that he imposes on himself."[5]

Above all, a man discerning a vocation to the priesthood must *pray*, and we will take up this thread again in chapter 3, on prayer in the life of the priest.

[5] *Scintillae Ignatianae*, ed. Gábor Hevenesi, S.J. (Vienna: J. G. Schlegel, 1705), p. 157 (translation by author).

CHAPTER 2

The Mystery of the Priest

On the basis of his biblical studies, Martin Luther confidently declared that the New Testament does not know of a special priestly office. He pointed out that priestly terminology (*hiereus, archiereus, prosphora, thusia*) is applied to the Old Testament priests, to Jesus, and to the entire people of God. Special ministry in the Church is necessary, he said, but it is a human institution and arose out of mere practical necessity. Nowadays even some Catholic biblical scholars, such as Raymond Brown, agree on the lack of evidence for the ministerial priesthood in the New Testament. Nevertheless, even these scholars maintain that the ministerial priesthood's emergence in the Church as early as the end of the first century was not without divine initiative (*jure divino*, as the Council of Trent teaches).

THE BIBLICAL FOUNDATIONS OF THE NEW TESTAMENT PRIESTHOOD

From the studies of Yves Congar, André Feuillet, and Albert Vanhoye however, it is clear that far from testifying to its absence, the biblical terminology helps us to understand better the nature of the ministerial priesthood. In pagan religions and even in the Old Testament, there were many priests in their own right who offered animals and produce of the land rather than offering themselves for their own sacrifices and for those of the people. These priests mediated in their own name between the people and their gods. In contrast, the New Testament knows only one priest, one sacrifice, and one temple: Jesus Christ. Moreover, the entire body of the faithful participates in that one priesthood, one sacrifice, and one temple. Saint Peter exhorts his readers in this way:

> "Be yourselves built into a spiritual house, to be a holy priesthood, to offer spiritual sacrifices [*pneumatikas thusias*] acceptable to God through Jesus Christ ... you are a chosen race, a royal priesthood, a holy nation, God's own people, that you may declare the wonderful deeds of him who called you out of darkness into his marvelous light" (1 Pt 2:5, 9).

Thus, the Christian people, as a whole, is a royal priesthood chosen by God the Father for a twofold purpose: to offer spiritual sacrifices to God through the mediation of Christ and to proclaim the praises of God in the midst of the darkness of a sinful and unbelieving world.

We learn what spiritual sacrifice means from the Letter to the Romans: "I appeal to you therefore, brethren, by the mercies of God, to present your bodies as a living sacrifice [*thusian zosan*], holy and acceptable to God, which is your spiritual worship. Do not be conformed to this world but be transformed by the renewal of your mind, that you may prove what is the will of God, what is good and acceptable and perfect" (Rom 12:1–2). Spiritual sacrifice and spiritual worship, then, involve our living bodily selves, renewed and transformed, which we offer to God by uniting ourselves to God's will. And all this happens through Jesus Christ.

So at first sight it seems indeed that there is no place in the New Testament for what later will be called the ministerial priesthood. The entire body of the Church is priestly; every Christian performs the priestly service of offering his body to God and proclaiming His glorious deeds. Yet, Jesus chooses a special group to be called "apostles": "the Twelve"—for example, Judas Thaddeus and James, the "brother" of Jesus—and those associated with them after Jesus' Resurrection, such as Paul. They are the ones charged to preach the gospel, baptize, and forgive and retain sins. While every Christian has to offer himself as a living spiritual sacrifice, Paul describes the special vocation of the apostle for the Gentiles, which easily lends itself to describing the apostolic vocation in general: " But on some points I have written to you very boldly by way of reminder, because of the grace given me by God to be a minister [*leitourgon*] of Christ Jesus to the Gentiles in the priestly service [*hierourgounta*] of the gospel of God, so that the offering of the Gentiles [*prosphora ton ethnon*] may be acceptable, sanctified by the Holy Spirit (Rom 15:15–16)." Paul received the grace from God to be a public minister (*leitourgon*) of Jesus Christ; the term *leitourgos* would come to mean "liturgist" in a Christian context, one who performs a public celebration of divine worship that is centered on the gospel. The purpose of Paul's priestly service is to enable the (self-)offering of the Gentiles to be acceptable and sanctified by the Holy Spirit. While the priestly service of the Christian people is the presentation of their own selves to God as a living sacrifice through Christ, the apostle's priestly ministry is to make the self-offering of an entire community become acceptable and sanctified in the Holy Spirit. Note that "by the Holy Spirit" (Rom 15:16) and "through Jesus Christ" (1 Pet 2:5) are intimately connected: Christ's mediating role takes place in the Spirit.

Moreover, the priestly service of the gospel has a wider meaning than mere preaching. It takes place by words and actions, including the celebration of the Eucharist.

The priestly service of the apostle continues, to an extent, in the role of the ministerial priesthood carried out by the bishop and the priest.[1] Consequently, their work is not limited to the celebration of the Eucharist and of the other sacraments. Neither the bishop nor even the priest is simply a "sacramental minister". On different levels, the purpose of both is to build up a loving and worshipping community through preaching, sacramental ministry, and personal contact so that the eucharistic celebration may reach its threefold goal: (1) to build up more perfectly the Body of Christ; (2) to enable the members to unite their gift of self with the one perfect self-donation of Christ to the Father; and, to the extent that they are united in Christ, (3) to become through Him and with Him gifts to one another.

Later theological reflection has further elaborated the task of the ministerial priesthood vis-à-vis the priesthood of all the faithful. We will sketch out its most important insights.

1. In Persona Christi Capitis: *Representing the Church's Radical Dependence on Christ*

The Church is not self-sufficient: she does not exist in and by herself, but in a radical dependence on the person of Christ. She is the *pleroma* of Christ (Eph 1:23), a community of people joined together by Christ through the Holy Spirit and growing toward Christ. The Church is always in the process of being built up. She will reach her full

---

[1] But only to an extent, because the apostles were eyewitnesses to Christ while the bishops are not. The apostles are the foundations of the Church, and the bishops only heads of local churches.

measure of growth only at the point of eschatological fulfillment (Eph 4:15–16). Thus, in a sense, the whole Church
may be identified with Christ because she is the Body of
Christ insofar as her members are united by the Spirit
of Christ and thereby manifest His life to the world.

The identification with Christ, however, is incomplete,
and it is only one aspect of the mystery of the Church.
Besides the analogy "Body of Christ", Saint Paul uses met-
aphors that stress both the unity and distinction between
the Church and the person of Christ: Christ is the head
of His Body, the Church. He is the source of her life,
He has complete authority over her, and He is the model
and exemplar toward which the Church grows (Col 1:18;
2:9–10; Eph 4:15–16; 5:23).[2]

As the very nature of the Church is both spiritual and
visible (sacramental), it is to be expected *a priori* that what
is most essential to her, her dependence on the person of
Christ, also be expressed sacramentally. Thus it becomes
understandable that *the person of Jesus Christ*, Who constitutes and builds up the Church, is represented by *the person
of the ministerial priest*. Vatican II emphasizes that the ministerial priest (both bishop and presbyter) acts "*in persona
Christi Capitis*": "in the person of Christ the Head [of the
body of the Church]".[3] Therefore, the existence and function of the ministerial priesthood does not merely derive
from a practical sociological necessity (for example, every
organization needs leaders), but from the sacramental
nature of the Church. From this, two conclusions follow.

First, the service character of the ministerial priesthood
becomes evident. The Church does not exist for the sake
of the priests, but on the contrary, ministerial priests exist

---

[2] Another way to express the distinction between Christ and the Church is
with the image of the bride, to be discussed later.

[3] *Presbyterorum ordinis* (hereafter *PO*), no. 2; cf. also *Lumen gentium* (hereafter
LG), no. 21.

to serve the Church. It is through their preaching and celebration of the sacraments, especially the Eucharist, that the whole people of God is enabled to exercise her royal priesthood and her prophetic mission. The ministerial priest will function only until the end of time, but the royal priesthood of the faithful will unfold its perfection in the perfect state of the kingdom of God. Then we will no longer need sacramental signs, since we will see and worship God face to face. This self-effacing, transitional, and instrumental role constitutes the low and humble character of the ministerial priesthood.

Second, if the ministerial priest were but a delegate of the congregation of the faithful, appointed by them in order to act in their name and to do what in principle any other faithful could do, it would signify that the Church is self-sufficient, possessing all the gifts of the Spirit in herself and by herself.

The Catholic priest, however, stands in the line of apostolic succession. Thus, as he is sent by Christ and acting in His person, the function of the ministerial priest manifests that all that the Church has and is comes as a gift from the Father through His Son, Jesus Christ. The grandeur of the priest, then, consists in his role as the sacramental representation of Christ. Yet his grandeur is not his own: Christ has invested him with His own authority.

We need to specify further the meaning of the priest's sacramental representation in light of a contemporary controversy.

2. Doulos Iesou Christou: *Servant of Christ in Sacramental Representation*

Opposing Pope John Paul II's teaching that the priest is the sacramental representation of Christ, a number of theologians chose another way to describe the ministerial priest's vocation: he is the *doulos Iesou Christou* (the servant or slave of Jesus Christ), as Paul likes to refer to himself. Yet, in the New Testament, as well as in the tradition of the Church, the two terms clarify, rather than exclude, each other. The theologians supporting the term "servant" are right that the role of the priest, just as that of the apostle, is to be and to act as a servant, a slave, of Christ. What they fail to see, however, is the intrinsic connection between radical servanthood and sacramental representation. In Pope John Paul II's clarification on the latter, the complementarity of the two definitions comes to light. He writes that the phrase *in persona Christi* "means more than the offering 'in the name of' or 'in the place of' Christ. *In persona* means in specific sacramental identification with 'the eternal High Priest' who is the author and principal subject of this sacrifice of His, a sacrifice in which, in truth, nobody can take his place."[4]

This role of sacramental representation implies a most radical, freely accepted slavery to Christ. If the priest were merely a delegated servant of Christ, Christ could not be "the principal subject" of the sacramental action, since only His delegate is present. "Specific sacramental identification", however, means that the priest does not merely act as a messenger of the absent Christ; rather he freely allows Christ to expropriate his sacramental actions in such a way that Christ Himself acts through him. Is such an ontological dependence on Christ not a freely accepted slavery of the most radical type?

The combination of the sacramental model with that of the servant offers a better protection against misunderstanding the phrase "sacerdos, alter Christus" (the priest

---

[4]John Paul II, letter *Dominicae cenae* (February 24, 1980), no. 8.

is another Christ). Priests do not multiply Christ; they
are other persons than Christ. But in the sacramental
action, they are the living and free instruments of the one
Christ, Who is present as the "principal subject" of their
actions.[5] The existential acceptance of this role, then,
should lead on the one hand to a conscious effort on the
part of the priest to let Christ live and shine through his
person and daily life; on the other hand, he should resist
the constant temptation to confuse his own person with
that of Christ. Saint Bernard relates a story about a horse
carrying a prince. The horse thinks that all the honors
and the adulation are directed at him. Such a fool, writes
Bernard, is the bishop or priest who thinks that awe and
reverence are directed at his private person, rather than
at Christ, Whom he represents. It is indeed a sad experience to see a priest forcing himself to appear holier than
he really is. But if he thinks he is supposed to be Christ,
what else can he do? Unfortunately, in order to avoid this
temptation, many well-meaning clergymen after Vatican
II seem to have fallen into the opposite trap. They strive
eagerly to get rid of all the "mystique" of the priesthood,
since *Lumen gentium* famously declared that all baptized
Christians have the same Christian dignity. Therefore,
they reduce their priesthood to carrying out certain
(temporary) functions, and as soon as they finish the sacramental rite, they humbly and gladly disappear into the
Christian community, which, to their mind, ought to
become more and more self-directed. As a result of this
misunderstanding, the postconciliar Church in some
places came very close to the democratic assembly of a
Protestant church.

A wise spiritual director used to tell his seminarians,
"Kneel down every day before your priesthood." Kissing

<hr>

[5] John Paul II, encyclical letter *Ecclesia de eucharistia* (April 17, 2003), no. 29.

the stole before putting it on might achieve a similar effect. We must learn to live this paradox: our participation in the priesthood of Christ should transform and define our whole personal existence and, at the same time, nourish in us the awareness that our priesthood remains forever an undeserved gift we have received for the sake of serving others.

Saint Bernard often uses the image of bridegroom and bride for the relationship between Christ and the Church, with the image of John the Baptist for the priest. John the Baptist came to prepare the way for Christ, and the greatest moment of his life came when he pointed him out: "Behold the Lamb of God, who takes away the sin of the world" (Jn 1:29). John is the God-sent matchmaker. His joy is fulfilled when he hears the joyous cry of the Bridegroom who has found his bride and found her a virgin. He must decrease, and Christ must increase (Jn 3:29–30). According to Bernard, the vocation of the priest is similar. He leads the souls to Christ and rejoices in their intimate encounter rather than standing between them.

Our priesthood, then, serves the priesthood of all the faithful. We enable our people to receive and activate their priesthood by baptizing them, nourishing their faith, and making present for them the eternal sacrifice of Christ, so that both we, ministerial priests, and the priestly people of God may offer Christ and ourselves to the Father through Him, with Him, and in Him. Saint Paul also expresses his priestly vocation in these terms: "I feel a divine jealousy for you, for I betrothed you to Christ to present you as a pure bride to her one husband" (2 Cor 11:2).

THE SACRAMENT OF HOLY ORDERS

The Sacrament of Holy Orders imparts to the ordinand the power for carrying out his ministry and offers him the

grace of the Holy Spirit for living and acting in the way
that befits his office. The bishop receives the fullness of the
sacrament; the presbyter only participates in that fullness
and carries out his ministry in submission to a bishop. The
deacon is ordained to assist the presbyters and to serve in
various ways the people of God.

According to the Acts of the Apostles and the two letters to Timothy, Church office in the apostolic age was
conferred by the imposition of hands (Acts 6:6; 1 Tim
4:14; 2 Tim 1:6).[6] I quote here the most detailed text in
which Paul exhorts Timothy: "I remind you to rekindle
(*anazopurein*) the gift of God (*to charisma tou theou*) that is
within you through the laying on of my hands; for God
did not give us a spirit of timidity but a spirit of power
and love and self-control" (2 Tim 1:6–7). Timothy, one
of Paul's closest collaborators and his representative in
Ephesus, received his mission and authority from Paul
by the imposition of Paul's hands. According to 1 Tim
4:14, the rite included a "prophetic utterance" that accom-
panied the laying on of hands by several presbyters. The
charism Timothy received marks him as one appointed
by the Holy Spirit (Acts 20:28). It remains permanently in
him but needs to be rekindled from time to time in order
to assure that Timothy carries out his mission with courage, love, and self-control.

The essential sign of ordination, then, goes back to
the apostolic Church and has remained basically the same
throughout the ages. Later reflection clarified that the
charism of holy orders lasts until the death of the recipient.
In other words, along with baptism and confirmation, this

---

[6] In the first two centuries A.D., the words *presbuteros* and *episkopos* were often
used synonymously for "church office" without a clear distinction between
bishop and presbyter.

sacrament impresses a permanent seal upon the soul and is therefore unrepeatable. Its grace effect, however, may be weakened or lost by sin, though it may still be regained through contrition and the reception of the Sacrament of Penance.

Regarding holy orders, the Magisterium of the Church has only defined that the sacramental character, just like that of baptism and confirmation, is permanent, indelible, and unrepeatable. There has been no further explication on what the sacramental character actually is. The prevailing traditional theological opinion holds to its Christological character: it conforms the recipient to Christ the High Priest. Yet a number of contemporary theologians have criticized its mystical and ontological interpretation. This, in their view, contributed to the "clericalization" of the priestly ministry, an elevation of the priest to an exclusive higher caste marking him as an allegedly holier type of Christian. In order to counter this error, these theologians began to "demythologize" the character and to reduce it to the mark of an officeholder in the Church. Almost inevitably, such a functional view of the priesthood led to practical consequences. "If I am an officeholder, why do I have to remain a priest until I die? If I think I can be of greater use to the Church in another job, is it not reasonable to change jobs? As a bonus, if I quit the ministry, I can marry, enjoy the blessing of a wife and children. In today's world, mobility and readiness to change alone assure satisfaction." Many a priest has justified his departure from his ministry on such or similar grounds.

Joseph Ratzinger gives a biblically grounded Christological interpretation of the priestly character.[7] Jesus is the One Who has been sent by the Father. His mission is not

---

[7] "Biblical Foundations of Priesthood", *Origins*, October 18, 1990: 310–14.

a function but defines His entire existence. He sends His entire Church to evangelize the world, but He sends bishops and priests with His own authority. They participate, to varying degrees, in the very mission of Christ. Therefore, their mission is not a job, but defines their entire existence. After their ordination, there is no time in their day and in their lives when they can take a vacation from their priesthood. They may engage in different secular activities—some of them compatible with their priestly vocation, others incompatible—but even when they eat, recreate, or rest, they always remain the ones whom Jesus has chosen and sent to represent Him. Thus, priesthood is not merely their function but has been imprinted on their very being, a real ontological change. On the other hand, the forming of an exclusive and status-conscious priestly caste is totally opposed to the mission of the Servant of God. He is sent precisely to serve rather than to dominate. The priest's mission is threefold, just as Christ's: to shepherd (king), to teach (prophet), and to offer sacrifice (priest).

THE THREEFOLD MISSION OF THE PRIEST

1. Shepherd

The grace of the sacrament enables the priest to live and carry out his mission, which shares in the threefold mission of Christ: king, prophet, and priest. In His earthly life, Christ rejected all the efforts of the people to make Him a political and military leader, a king in the mold of David. When He entered Jerusalem before His passion, the crowd believed that He had finally accepted the royal claim and would now begin His glorious reign. They were entirely unprepared for His execution on the Cross. Most likely, even His own disciples did not understand the divine irony of the Passion until after His Resurrection. The mocking gestures of Pilate as he seated Jesus on his own bench and declared before the people, "Behold your king", and his bitter insistence on the title he had hung above Jesus' head on the Cross in three languages, "Jesus of Nazareth, King of the Jews", in fact revealed the truth. Pilate, unawares, proclaimed to the world the divine plan. It is on the Cross that Jesus became enthroned king of Israel and, through this, king of the entire world. This kingship fulfilled the royal claim of the house of David by turning it upside down when Jesus pronounced His last words on the Cross: "It is finished" (*tetelestai*, Jn 19:30). As Jesus completed all His free acts of obedience on earth, His humanity has become a totally pliable and free instrument of God's will. After His Resurrection and the outpouring of the Holy Spirit, Jesus the man began His rule as king of the universe, visible only through the eyes of faith. Throughout history, He gathers His people into the one family of God and unites them to His glorified body. The first apostles enter into the fullness of Christ's kingdom through their martyrdom. Only then do they become powerful intercessors for the Church on earth; only then does Peter begin to carry the burden of all the churches through the successive line of the bishops of Rome.

How can any shepherd, bishop, or priest imagine for himself any other way of exercising leadership in the Church beside that of the apostles? How else but to gather together Christ's scattered sheep, to bind the wounds of the sick, to go after the stray, to embrace those whom the world despises, to preserve their purity of faith against the tidal waves of the all-powerful zeitgeist? All this is consuming zeal, a gradual laying down of one's life for the sheep.

When Peter exhorts the readers of his first letter, which was probably written during a time of persecution, to rejoice in their shared sufferings with Christ, he provides an image of the ideal presbyter:

> So I exhort the elders [presbyters] among you, as a fellow elder [presbyter] and a witness of the sufferings of Christ as well as a partaker in the glory that is to be revealed. Tend the flock of God that is in your charge, not by constraint but willingly, not for shameful gain but eagerly, not as domineering over those in your charge but being examples to the flock. And when the chief Shepherd is manifested you will obtain the unfading crown of glory (1 Pet 5:1–4).

Obviously, the ministry of shepherding can only be understood in close relationship with the tasks of preaching and sanctification. But first a community must be gathered and organized in such a way that it can be taught and sanctified. At the same time, the teaching and sacramental ministry further builds up the community into the Body of Christ and increases their active love for one another and for those outside. This work needs an organizing, supervising, and inspiring authority, and when good example and exhortation are spurned, the bishop and priest may have to take a stand and warn about the effects of going contrary to the Body of Christ.

The Christian community should be formed and governed to ensure the most favorable conditions for its sanctification. Authority, laws, duties, and rights in the community need to be practiced and respected in such a way that they serve this one purpose: to build up the flock in truth, love, and holiness.[8] As Peter cautioned, neither

---

[8] Cf. *LG*, no. 27.

the bishop in the diocese nor the priest in the parish should exercise his leadership in a dictatorial way, "domineering over" the flock (1 Pet 5:3); rather, he should apply the principle of subsidiarity in his work, so that he does not directly do tasks that someone else could do with more competence. Faced with so many responsibilities, the priest knows that he cannot do his job by himself. He must search for all the competent laypeople he can find—not only financial experts and architects, but also people with ordinary, or extraordinary, spiritual gifts. Many different lay ministries flourish in good parishes. They specialize in the care of the poor and the sick, in liturgy, and in religious education. They counsel engaged and married couples and help the divorced. The number of these ministries is still increasing. These multifaceted and differentiated activities call for a more demanding, and more sophisticated, priestly leadership. Enlisting the active cooperation of others, coordinating their activities, advising and encouraging them, is a much greater challenge than the one-man show of old. While we unfortunately still see too many instances of the authoritarian pastor, at the opposite extreme, some priests and bishops misunderstand the demands of the postconciliar era; they abandon the principle of one-man responsibility and allow the parish staff to go their own way, without providing guidance and direction. If a pastor or bishop shifts responsibility to others for what is going on in his parish or diocese, the mistake is as serious as if he had tried to do everything by himself. After all, he remains *the* shepherd who will have to give an account to God for each of his sheep. His leadership will consist primarily in respecting, inspiring, supervising, and coordinating various charisms for the good of the whole community.[9]

[9] Cf. *LG*, no. 27; *Christus dominus* (hereafter *CD*), no. 1620; *PO*, no. 6.

In the Church, the subject-superior relationship (parishioner-pastor, priest-bishop, bishop-pope) is always embedded in, and ordained to, the more fundamental relationship of cooperation and fraternal communion. This is expressed in many ways by the Council documents: the pope is head of the episcopal college, but also brother to the other bishops; the bishop is a father but also a friend and brother to his priests; likewise, the pastor is a father to his faithful but also a brother and friend to his parishioners, who share the same Christian dignity and life. The distinction between subject and superior is temporary, valid only for the time of the Church's earthly pilgrimage. But the communion of love, which this authority builds up, remains forever.

A religious or parish community that becomes a communion of love is a tremendous force to inspire society. Think of the early Middle Ages: Benedictine communities, establishing themselves among semi-barbarian tribes, tamed and educated the people around them, teaching literacy, religion, and agriculture and demonstrating how slave and freeman, people from hostile tribes and different languages, can live in harmony. A Christian community is always open, attracts and welcomes everyone, nurtures and teaches children, blesses marriages, heals the sick, and buries the dead.

To the extent that she is allowed by civil authorities, the Church intends to be present also in the public life of society, both on the national and international level. We mention here only two examples. After the Second World War, prominent Catholic leaders—Konrad Adenauer, the German chancellor; Alcide de Gasperi, the Italian prime minister; Robert Schuman, the French minister of foreign affairs—with the encouragement of Pope Pius XII, laid down the foundations of what is now the European

Union. Today in Africa, the Catholic Church is often the voice of the conscience of countries that suffer under corrupt leadership.

2. Prophet and Teacher

Jesus is not only the Shepherd King Who gives His life for the sheep, but He is also *the* Prophet. Relying on Moses' prophecy in Deuteronomy 18:18, Israel expected the fulfillment of God's promises in the form of a new prophet, a new Moses. Jesus in fact compares His destiny to that of the prophets who were rejected—and sometimes killed—by their own countrymen (Mt 23:34–36). The Gospels, especially Matthew, show the fulfillment of a prophet's destiny in Jesus as the new Moses. Jesus is, however, more than *a* prophet; He is *the* Prophet because, while Moses could see only the back of God (Ex 33:18–23), Jesus alone, as the only-begotten Son of the Father, sees God Himself, and reveals to us God's inmost mystery: the loving communion of the Father and the Son in the Holy Spirit. Thus, instead of merely transmitting words from God, Jesus *is* the Word, the definitive and total self-revelation of God to man. This self-revelation prepares those who accept it in faith for the sacrifice of the Cross and Resurrection, in which Jesus' revelation reaches both its fullness and its self-authentication. There is no divine revelation beyond the person, the words, and the actions of Jesus Christ. But as a divine-human reality, this revelation of person, words, and actions transcends all time and is present to all of history, while remaining always new, all-powerful, and inexhaustible.

Christ entrusts this revelation to the apostles and promises them His own presence in the Holy Spirit, Who introduces them to all truths. Therefore, Vatican II, opposing the historical distortion of the episcopal office into a chiefly administrative function and of the presbyters into a mere sacramental role, stresses *that the primary duty and task of bishops and priests is to proclaim the Gospel.*[10] Dependent on the episcopal order, the priesthood shares in the authority with which Christ Himself constitutes, sanctifies, and rules His Body.[11] It follows that "priests, as co-workers with their bishops, have the primary duty of proclaiming the gospel of God to all."[12]

Note Vatican II's emphasis that the duty of priests and bishops is to preach the gospel not just to faithful church-goers, but to everyone, as Jesus commanded: "Go into all the world and preach the gospel to the whole creation" (Mk 16:15).[13] The ministry of the Church is essentially missionary; the forms of this mission will vary from place to place (information services, radio, TV programs, publications, and different forms of dialogue). Priests and bishops, however, very often feel overwhelmed by the burden of their own people. They often ask, "I can't even do justice to my obligations *within* my parish (diocese)—how could I go beyond it?" A permanent missionary activity may be impossible for the pastor himself, but he can motivate and utilize the missionary zeal of many lay Christians and underused permanent deacons to reach out beyond the institutional boundaries.

Pastors have to proclaim "the whole mystery of Christ",[14] not only those themes that are attractive to a contemporary audience. One of the great temptations for the preacher who wants to ingratiate himself to his audience is to "edit" the

---

[10] Cf. *LG*, no. 25; *CD*, nos. 7, 12–14.
[11] *PO*, no. 2.
[12] *PO*, no. 4.
[13] *PO*, no. 4.
[14] *CD*, no. 12.

Bible by omitting difficult texts or by paraphrasing them so skillfully that the hard sayings of Jesus are reduced to harmless clichés. Obviously, those who always speak about the frightening judgment of God equally falsify the gospel. The gospel must always be presented as *euangelion*, good news, but the Cross and the Resurrection can only be understood together, as one indivisible mystery. There is no suffering for a Christian that cannot be illuminated by the sure hope of the resurrection, nor is there any Christian joy that does not call for the acceptance of the cross in some form.

The preacher must address issues of social injustice, the violations of the right to life for the unborn and for the elderly, and other immoral laws or immoral actions of the government, but he should not take sides on merely political matters in which no evangelical or natural moral value is at stake. The concrete ways in which moral principles should be applied ought to be left to competent politicians.

For the pastor of an affluent community, the strong temptation is to keep silent or rarely speak about social justice issues. If he speaks about the problems of poverty, it is usually with regard to giving food and clothes to the poor. He is afraid that if he preaches on the principles of Catholic social teaching, he will be a labeled socialist or even a Communist, and the donations to the parish and the poor will thereby dry up. Yet we have the grave obligation to present our people with the gospel of Christ in its integrity. We should point out that the Church opposes both Communism and laissez-faire capitalism—the former because the Church rejects class struggle and upholds the right to private property as a necessary means to assure the freedom of the citizens, and the latter because she does not subordinate the right to private property to the common good of society. She does not consider human work merely as merchandise to be bought strictly according to the laws of the market; nor does she consider any moral consideration an illegitimate intrusion into the sacrosanct supply-demand operation of the "invisible hand". The words of Pope Paul VI in the encyclical *Populorum progressio* are as relevant today as they were during its publication in 1967:

> "He who has the goods of this world and sees his brother in need and closes his heart to him, how does the love of God abide in him?" Everyone knows that the Fathers of the Church laid down the duty of the rich toward the poor in no uncertain terms. As St. Ambrose put it: "You are not making a gift of what is yours to the poor man, but you are giving him back what is his. You have been appropriating things that are meant to be for the common use of everyone. The earth belongs to everyone, not to the rich." These words indicate that the right to private property is not absolute and unconditional.
>
> No one may appropriate surplus goods solely for his own private use when others lack the bare necessities of life. In short, "as the Fathers of the Church and other eminent theologians tell us, the right of private property may never be exercised to the detriment of the common good." When "private gain and basic community needs conflict with one another," it is for the public authorities "to seek a solution to these questions, with the active involvement of individual citizens and social groups."[15]

We can relieve the tension in the minds of our affluent parishioners by pointing out that the Church does not tell them to distribute their superfluous wealth in the form of direct handouts to the poor. That would shortly lead to the collapse of any modern society. There are countless ways

[15] *Populorum progressio*, no. 23 (March 26, 1967).

the rich can contribute to the common good: providing job opportunities with decent pay, establishing charitable foundations for various needs, providing scholarships to deserving poor students, establishing health care centers for the uninsured, improving schools in poor areas, fostering small enterprises by providing what are called microeconomic loans, and so on.

Instead of constantly hammering into them the horrors of eternal damnation, it is helpful to remind parishioners of God's rich and immense generosity, which invites our responsive imitation of that generosity by turning our lives and wealth into service.

Good preaching is an exercise of the gift of prophecy: the preacher discovers and sheds the light of God's Word on the "vulnerable" spots of the faithful's soul—the cracks in the soul's armor where grace can penetrate. It may be an event, ordinary or extraordinary, a great joy or a great sorrow, a loss or a gift, a failure or success, an upheaval, or a pricking thorn in the soul or the body. The preacher has to think and feel with the audience in order to find in the readings the right words for shedding light upon a concrete situation and on the response God would expect from the listeners.

The lives and writings of the saints and saintly people, of Church Fathers like Saint Bernard, Augustine, and Gregory the Great, inspire and help many contemporary preachers to speak about the mysteries of our faith. Nevertheless, the most important factor in preparing an effective homily is the personal, spiritual experience of the priest: his prayers, his daily meditation, and his sensitivity to the working of God's grace in his own life. In one way or another, he must have experienced the truth of what he is speaking about. He might preach in a very simple way, but if the congregation feels that his whole person stands behind what he says, some people will be affected. There is a mysterious connection between the level of depth in the speaker and in the listener. Words uttered from the soul's surface will usually only reach the surface of the listener's heart. However, what comes from deep personal conviction may reach a similar depth in the listener. The mysteries of faith, however, have a width, depth, and height that infinitely surpass the limits of our personal experiences. Therefore, our faith and preaching must transcend these limits.

The valid administration of the sacraments requires only a minimum of personal involvement on the part of the priest;[16] that is, he must intend to perform an ecclesial act rather than a merely personal one. In the ministry of preaching, however, the words of Scripture are actualized as the Word of God to address the congregation here and now through the faith of the preacher. If the priest first listens to the Word, applies it to himself, and accepts being judged and changed by the Word, his preaching will be sincere and reach his listeners. Yet it will produce fruit only in those who have opened up their hearts to God's inner Word, Who speaks to and changes the heart.

Saint Bernard has left us a beautiful summary of the theology of preaching in his discourse on conversion, which is addressed to the students of the University of Paris. It deepens and expands eloquently what I have said above:

> You have come here, I am sure, to hear the word of God. Certainly no other reason for such an eager crowd of you to be here comes to my mind. I altogether approve of

---

[16] Of course, a priest should also enter personally into the sacramental act. He should live what he celebrates. The Church's prayers for the penitent, the sick, the bride and groom, and the newly baptized or confirmed, as well as the eucharistic prayer, should become the expression of his own personal prayer.

this desire, and I too rejoice in this praiseworthy zeal. For blessed are they who hear the word of God—if they keep it. Blessed are those who are mindful of his commandments, as long as they do them. Indeed, He has the words of eternal life, and the time is coming—may it be this moment too!—when the dead will hear His voice, and they who hear it will live: for indeed, life is in His will. And if you want to know, what He wills is our conversion. Just listen to Him: "Is my will the death of the wicked," says the Lord, "and not rather that he be converted and live?" From these words we clearly recognize that there is no true life for us but in conversion, nor does the entrance to life open up in any other way, as the Lord Himself says: "Unless you are converted and become like little children, you will not enter into the kingdom of heaven." And it is quite right that only little children should enter, since a tiny child drives them on who was born and given to us precisely for this. Therefore, I ask for a voice that the dead can hear, and when they hear it, live: for perhaps it is necessary to preach the good news even to those who are dead. And a short saying comes to mind, then, brief but dense, which the mouth of the Lord has spoken, as the Prophet declares: "You have said," he says, undoubtedly referring to the Lord his God, "Be converted, O sons of men." Nor is it at all inappropriate that conversion be demanded of the sons of men, since it is certainly necessary for sinners. For it is rather on the spirits above that the praise that suits the just has been enjoined, as the Prophet sings: "Praise your God, O Zion."

Furthermore, in my judgment one should not lightly pass over his saying, "You have said," nor should this be taken literally. For who would dare compare to human words what God is said to have said? In fact, the word of God is living and effective, and his voice has splendor and power. For "He spoke, and they were made." He said, "[Let] there be light," and there was light. He said: "Be converted," and the sons of men were converted. Clearly, then, the conversion of souls is a work of the divine voice, not the human. Though Simon, son of John, was called by the Lord and instituted as a fisher of men for this very task, nevertheless even he works all night in vain and will catch nothing, until, casting his net at the Lord's word, he can take in an abundant multitude. May I too cast my net at this word today, that I may experience what has been written: "Behold, he will make his voice a mighty voice!" If I tell a lie, clearly that is something of my own. But perhaps even when I seek what is mine and not what belongs to Jesus Christ it will be taken to be my voice and not the voice of the Lord. Besides, even if I do speak of the justice of God and seek the glory of God, it is still necessary to hope and ask for success from him and him alone, that he may "render his voice a mighty voice." I advise you, then, to prick the ears of your heart to this interior voice, to strive to hear God speaking within you rather than the man speaking outside you. For that is the voice of splendor and power, the voice that stirs the wastelands, uncovers the hidden recesses, and shakes off the torpor of souls.

Nor does it really take much work to hear this voice; it takes work, rather, to stop your ears lest you hear. Truly, the voice presents itself, forces itself upon us, and never stops knocking at each man's door. For he says, "Forty years I was so close to this generation, and said: They always wander off in their hearts." He is still right with us, he still speaks, and perhaps there is no one who listens. He still says: "They wander off in their hearts"; Wisdom still cries out in the streets: "Return to your heart, transgressors." This is certainly how the Lord begins speaking. . . .[17]

Even if the preacher proclaims not himself but the Word of God, he should ask and pray that the Lord may "render

---

[17] Saint Bernard, *Ad clericos de conversione*, in *Opera omnia*, vol. 4, trans. Fr. Stephen Cregg, O.Cist. (Rome: Editiones Cistercienses, 1966), pp. 69–72.

His voice a mighty voice", the "voice of power and light", in order to work inside the hearers by enlightening their souls and by giving them life.

Bernard subverts the conviction of the average Christian who believes that God "speaks" to us rarely, if ever, and therefore gives up the effort to tune in to Him. According to Bernard: "the voice presents itself, forces itself upon us, and never stops knocking at each man's door." We are the ones who make a real effort to stop our ears. We do not want to hear Him because the divine voice calls us back to our own hearts, where we are faced with the filth and disorder that covers up the divine image within us.

People shaped by today's culture either do not know much about sin or simply consider the entire notion outdated and irrelevant. Any preacher who would start his sermon by attempting to convince an urban audience of their sinfulness would hit a wall of indifference or even outright scorn. But if a contemporary preacher would address a youth group in terms such as these—"Return to your heart. Ask yourself, 'Do I have peace in my heart, do I connect with people, or do I rather feel restless, lonely, at times a stranger to myself, to my family and friends?'"—he could wake up most listeners. By graphically describing the experience of loneliness and alienation, we can then show our listeners that its root is our estrangement from God and the suppression of our most noble desires.

It is important not to indulge *exclusively* in moralizing homilies. We would just increase the audience's alienation from "organized religion". Christian morality is always a response to the loving, saving actions of God. We should never lose sight of the *euangelion*, the good news of Christianity. The crucified and risen Lord calls us not just to be reconciled with our Creator, but to come home to the house of our Father Who waits for us, runs to embrace us, and slaughters the fattened calf for us. We become children of God the Father, members of His incarnate Son Jesus, and therefore brothers and sisters to each other. All this happens, not by means of a divine legal adoption agency, but through the Holy Spirit Who re-creates us, changes our very being into the likeness of the first-begotten Son. In fact, we are already taken up in this life—the life of the Trinity; we praise, thank, and petition the Father with and through Jesus Christ while the Holy Spirit Himself prays in us. This share in the trinitarian life of infinite and eternal love through the sacrifice of Christ is the heart of our faith, yet how rarely we preach about it! An equally essential topic for preaching is the Eucharist, which (or rather, Who) takes us up into the sacrifice of Christ and invites us to unite our bodies to His body, our soul to His soul and divinity. In this way, we ourselves become a gift for the Father and for our neighbors. Christian morality, then, is both simple and demanding: we learn to live as *what* we are, children of God, united with Jesus in the mystery of His dying and rising.

We rarely preach about what these mysteries of sharing in Christ's sacrifice and trinitarian life mean for us. Perhaps this is because we feel that our congregation would not really understand these teachings; or perhaps it is because even for us, these themes do not mean much more than some abstract dogma—that is, they are not existentially attractive. What may help us is to face our own future: What shall we do in heaven if we are bored now to think about sharing Christ's life with His Father? How then shall we be able to become a gift in our entire being, a gift for the Father and for our brothers and sisters? If we take seriously the dangerous possibility of being eternally bored in heaven (which is not too removed from being in hell!), we will also discover the medicine: daily reading of Sacred

Scripture and daily meditation on it. This practice is more likely to produce good homilies than a late Saturday night spent reading the most recent Bible commentaries in the hopes of churning out some half-digested information, spiced up with a funny story to keep the congregation awake. If we have a daily conversation with Jesus, we will learn to know Him, love Him, and desire to be with Him. This desire will enlarge our soul, and our enlarged soul will long for Him even more intensely. Homilies born from such a fire will warm up at least some, or perhaps many, freezing souls.[18] We should also gather as many "foretaste experiences" of heaven as we can: a loving family celebration; the joy of giving and receiving gifts, which are signs of sincere love and appreciation; a father or mother embracing a wayward teenage son; your First Communion when you knew that Christ Himself was feeding you with His love and life; the celebration of a wedding; the peace on the face of a saintly person who has just passed away; and innumerable other events, both small and great. We must show to our people that heaven is close; it can penetrate our daily lives, just as hell is anticipated in the experience of malicious, inveterate sinners.

Even when the main topic of our homily is a moral issue, we should talk about it in the light of both reason and revelation. For instance, abortion is wrong not simply because it is a mother killing her own child, but also because it opposes the infinite love of the Father Who had wanted to raise that child as His own son or daughter; it ignores the fact that God the Son gave His own life so that this child could live forever, and it is deaf to the Spirit's warning in the mother's heart. However, we should also

---

[18] Of course, good recent and old commentaries are valuable, but only as an earlier, remote preparation rather than a frantic search for ideas at the last hour.

point out the often-huge gap between the objective evil of abortion and the mother's moral awareness of it: many women truly did not know what they were doing. And even if they did know, God's mercy reaches out to them.

A few words are in order about the delivery and the length of the homily. Some priests are afraid that official liturgical greetings fail to wake up the congregation. In order to create a conversational tone, they begin with "good morning". The congregation may conclude from this that the priest is a really down-to-earth, friendly guy. At the same time, however, the official greeting before the Gospel, "the Lord be with you", loses its meaning and turns into a mere formality. The original Latin phrase *Dominus vobiscum* has a double meaning: "The Lord is with you" and "the Lord be with you." The homilist expresses his hope that the Lord is already in the heart of his listeners and that by his homily, the Lord's presence will be intensified and more effective within them. "Good morning" or "good evening" lowers the expectation of hearing something sacred and solemn.

A famous professor of homiletics summed up his advice in these words: First, stir up interest; second, say something; third, finish before you lose your audience.

If you begin with "Holy Mother Church celebrates today the last Sunday of the liturgical year", the congregation may quickly conclude that they are not going to hear anything worth their attention. Rather, start with an interesting experience, your own or someone else's, that wakes up your audience. If you read, meditate, and live the Scriptures, most of the time you will find in your life an experience that naturally connects with a biblical theme.

As we deliver the message of the homily, we do well to keep in mind what we are doing: following in the footsteps of the entire Christian tradition. We show to our people that what God did once in history, He continues to do every day in our souls. We should pray, before preaching, that the Holy Spirit, Who alone can make our words effective, may accompany our external words by His internal word in the hearers' hearts.

The unprepared preacher usually has a hard time finishing the homily. He seems close to landing several times, but just when we think he will stop, he takes off again because he cannot find the concluding words. Prepare the concluding lines well in advance!

3. Sacramental Minister

In preaching, the homilist bears witness to the Word of God, but he cannot ensure (only hope and ask) that the Holy Spirit will accompany his words by inspiring the hearts of listeners. The dynamics of the sacramental ministry, however, are different because the sacramental action of the Church is infallibly connected to Christ. Evidently, the ritual act does not impose on us the acceptance of grace, but it assures that here and now Christ offers us His grace and, in the Eucharist, His full personal presence. As the Church explains with a concise formula, the sacraments confer grace *ex opere operato*, that is, by the performance of the sacramental ritual. We must make it clear that this phrase has nothing to do with magic. In magic, the magician tries to *force* a superior power to obey his will. In sacramental actions, the minister *obeys* Christ's will and asks Christ to sanctify the recipient. As said before, the infallible offer of grace does not automatically sanctify but appeals to the freedom of the recipient. The words of the Book of Revelation beautifully illustrate the personal aspect of the offer of grace: "Behold, I stand at the door and knock; if any one hears my voice and opens

the door, I will come in to him and eat with him, and he
with me" (3:20).

For a fuller understanding of how the *ex opere operato*
principle "works", we can study the way Jesus forgives,
sanctifies, heals, and raises the dead in the Gospels. The
scene of the raising of Lazarus from the tomb is especially
helpful. Before Jesus acts, He prays to His Father: "Father,
I thank you that you have heard me. I knew that you
always hear me, but I have said this on account of the people standing by, that they may believe that you sent me"
(Jn 11:41–42). In the Gospel of John, we see the paradox:
the Son is one with the Father, yet He constantly con-
verses with Him, doing and saying only what the Father
tells Him. Thus, we may assume that every saying and
every deed of Jesus is the fruit of His prayerful dialogue
with His Father.[19] In the story of Lazarus, the commanding words of Jesus reveal the silent response of the Father
to Jesus' prayer: "Lazarus, come out" (11:43).

According to Schillebeeckx, we discover here the pattern of every sacramental event. The priest, as representative of the Church and Christ, transmits the prayer of
the Church through Jesus to the Father and imparts to the
recipient the sanctifying action of the Father through
Christ. Here are a few examples. In the Sacrament of Baptism, the prayer over the baptismal water expresses the
petition of the Church for sanctification through Christ to
the Father. The words of baptism itself ("N., I baptize you
in the name of the Father and the Son and the Holy Spirit.
Amen") effect in the baptizand the sanctifying response of
the Father through Christ. In the Eucharist, the words
of the epiclesis present the Church's request through Jesus

---

[19] According to a very credible exegetical opinion, the "Amen sayings" of
Jesus are the Synoptic equivalent of the Johannine dialogues between Father
and Son. The "Amen" of Jesus demonstrates that His words are the conclusion
of an interior listening to His Father.

to the Father, asking that the Father may send the Holy Spirit to consecrate through Christ the Church's offerings into the Body and Blood of Christ. The words of the Consecration, then, carry out the Father's response. The Sacrament of Reconciliation also includes this twofold ecclesial-trinitarian movement: the deprecative (petitioning) formula "Through the ministry of the Church may God give you pardon and peace" is followed by the declaration: "I absolve you from your sins in the name of the Father and of the Son and of the Holy Spirit. Amen."

The ideal way for the priest to celebrate the sacraments is to live personally what he celebrates ritually. Concretely, it means that he should pray the rites while trying to mean the words he says. Thus, with the help of the Holy Spirit, the priest will be united with the intentions of Christ expressed in the rites of the Church. He will pray with Christ for the new birth of the baptizand, for the fullness of the Holy Spirit in the confirmand, for the forgiveness and healing of the penitent, and for forgiveness and strength for the sick that they may unite their sufferings with the suffering Christ. In the priestly ordination, the bishop prays that the new minister may represent Christ not only with his ritual activities but also with his entire life. In the celebration of marriage, the priest, as the official witness of the Church, will ask the Father through His Son that the couple may love and serve each other as Christ loved the Church and gave His life for her.

Both the shepherding and preaching activities of the priest are ordained toward the fruitful celebration of the sacraments, which culminate in the Eucharist. In the Eucharist, Christ Himself is present in His sacrifice, to which the faithful can unite their own gift of self and thus become one body and one spirit with Christ and with each other, as well as a pleasing gift to the Father. However, the Eucharist is not only the climax of the Church's liturgical life but also the fountainhead of all her grace, as well as of her charitable and evangelizing mission. Saint John Chrysostom exhorts his people to return from receiving Communion as "lions breathing fire" so that through receiving Christ's eucharistic Body they may recognize and feed the Body of Christ in the poor.[20] Catholic morality is profoundly eucharistic. If the faithful are united with Christ in the sacrament, and through Christ with each other, they should live with Him and glorify Him in their lives.

Surveying the areas of priestly activity, we have seen that the priesthood is ministerial in a twofold way: both for Christ and for the people of God. The clergy serve Christ *for the sake of the people*. They make Christ present in His word, in His sanctifying actions, and in His sacrifice. They do all of this for the people of God so that the faithful may actualize their "royal priesthood", the offering of themselves in union with Christ to the Father. The Second Vatican Council's Decree on the Ministry and Life of Priests, *Presbyterorum ordinis*, summarizes in one condensed sentence the role and purpose of the priestly mission: "Exercising the office of Christ, the Shepherd and Head, and according to their share of his authority, priests, in the name of the bishop, gather the family of God together as a brotherhood enlivened by one spirit. Through Christ they lead them in the Holy Spirit to God the Father."[21]

A New Evangelization?

The last three popes, Saint John Paul II, Benedict XVI, and Francis, have each called the entire Church—every

---

[20] *Homilies on the Gospel of John*, trans. Charles Marriott, rev. Kevin Knight, homily 46.3, https://www.newadvent.org/fathers/240146.htm.

[21] *Presbyterorum ordinis*, no. 6.

Christian, but especially the clergy—to the urgent task of a "New Evangelization".[22] A synod of bishops dealt with this theme, a pontifical council was established for its promotion, and a number of articles were published to spell out its conditions, goals, and methods. Here I would like to point out only one of the New Evangelization's essential features—the readiness for martyrdom—without which it could not succeed.

Saint Paul, speaking to Timothy about his ordination, encourages him, "Take your share of suffering for the gospel in the power of God" (2 Tim 1:8). Today, Christianity is the most widely and consistently persecuted religion in most parts of the world. In the Western world, persecution takes the shape of ideological and legal pressure, which imposes upon judges, teachers, and doctors participation in certain practices—for example, same-sex marriage, transgender surgeries, abortion, or contraception—that are unacceptable to a Catholic conscience. In other parts of the world, persecution is more open and violent, such as the destruction or desecration of churches, as well as the incarceration, torture, and murder of Christians.

The Greek word *martus* means "witness", and in Christianity, martyrdom means witnessing to the truth of the faith in spite of suffering or death. The way a Christian lives and acts, suffers and dies, bears witness to the reality that what he lives and dies for is more precious than his earthly life. In our times, the term "martyrdom" has acquired an unsavory connotation because it evokes in many the image of suicide bombers. The large number of terrorists and their fanatic self-sacrifice does not serve as a

---

[22] Originally, "new evangelization" meant the re-evangelization of the West by presenting the Gospel in its beauty and power to a skeptical post-Christian culture. Today, however, it simply means the effort to find the most effective ways to evangelize every culture.

credible witness to their faith. Saint Clement of Alexandria
tells us that the Devil likes to ape God. For instance, the
myths of the pagan gods' intercourse with young virgins
on earth represent the Devil's version of Mary's virginal
conception of Jesus; by these stories, Satan attempts to
discredit the truth of the faith. We might not be far from
the truth if we interpret the martyrdom of suicide bombers
as a new diabolic effort to imitate and desecrate Christian
martyrdom. But the differences are evident. The suicide
bombers seek to murder innocent people whom they hate
by exploding themselves among them. The Christian martyrs do not seek martyrdom and do not hate their enemies;
they do not commit suicide or murder, and they pray that
their executioners may be forgiven and obtain eternal life.
One seeks death, the other life. As Saint John says, Satan
"was a murderer from the beginning" (Jn 8:44).

Every proclamation of Christ must conform to the
apostolic preaching, not only in its content, but also in its
form, which prefers the gospel to one's life. In her martyrs,
the Church becomes fully transparent to Christ by showing His glory shining in our human weakness. Peter, a
stumbling block (*skandalon*) for Jesus in his earthly life, will
be able to represent Jesus as the rock foundation for the
Church only when he becomes ready to follow Jesus unto
the Cross (Mt 16:17–24; Jn 21:15–19). Ignatius of Antioch
is afraid that he will remain an empty voice unless he is
allowed to become a martyr; only then will his personality
be so transparent that he himself becomes "the word of
God".[23] Those Christians who saw Blandina, a young girl
martyred in an arena in second-century France, saw Christ

---

[23] *Epistle of Ignatius to the Romans*, ch. 2 (translation by author). See more
on apostolicity and martyrdom in William R. Farmer & Roch Kereszty, *Peter
and Paul in the Church of Rome: The Ecumenical Potential of a Forgotten Perspective*
(New York: Paulist, 1990), pp. 53–97.

Himself in her.[24] By giving up his life for Christ, the martyr becomes an effective sign that Christ is infinitely more valuable than his own self. Most preachers and missionaries are not called to martyrdom by blood, yet all of us encounter situations in which we have to choose between the truth of the gospel on the one hand and popularity, material benefits, or promotion on the other. In some sense, then, we are all called to martyrdom insofar as we ought to give up part of our lives for the sake of the gospel and thereby witness to its supreme truth.

[24] "They beheld with their outward eyes, in the form of their sister, him who was crucified for them" (Eusebius, *Historia Ecclesiae*, bk. 1, ch. 1, para. 41).

CHAPTER 3

Prayer and the Priest

THE BEGINNINGS

Unlike in the priesthood of the Old Testament, which was the birthright of the sons of the house of Aaron, the prophet-priests of the New Testament, like the prophets of the Old, are individually chosen and personally called by God. Paul describes his apostolic vocation with the words of the prophetic call of Jeremiah: God set him apart from his mother's womb and called him through his grace.[1] Regardless of how the call reaches the person, whether awakened by a priest, a parent, or a friend, it will always penetrate the inmost depths of his soul and surface in his consciousness in the form of a question, a desire, a frightening burden, a sweet dream, or even an unshakeable certainty. Already at this point, the one who has become aware of the call should respond with prayer. If he ignores it and tries to mute it by throwing himself into the numbing noise of distractions or burying himself in work, God may still pursue him just as He did Jonah.

After a while, however, if the called one consistently ignores the Lord's voice, God may leave the man to his freedom and give up the chase. Even a loud protest to God is better than silence before His invitation. If someone

[1] Gal 1:15.

begins to fight God, enumerating all the obvious reasons why he should not become a priest or religious, God will fight back, and he should allow Him to overcome his resistance. The most insidious way of resisting God is assuring Him that you sincerely want to obey His will, whatever it might be, yet insisting that His call be "clear and unambiguous". One might remind God, for example, of Paul's vocation: he was knocked down to the ground by a blinding light. But God rarely obeys our whims or preconceptions and almost always surprises us. He spoke to Elijah in a gentle breeze (1 Kgs 19:12), and very often the loud noise of our cravings makes us deaf to His whispering.

As we surrender to the call, we should also accept the possibility that we are mistaken about it. But it will never be clarified unless we develop a regular prayer life, including confession, spiritual reading, and frequent or even daily participation in the Eucharist. Also of real importance is the selection of a capable spiritual director. The quality of our prayer in this preparatory stage will greatly influence our later priestly life and activities. Even at this point, God sees us connected with all those who will later be entrusted to our care. Our fight against temptations, as well as a generous renunciation of all that could hinder our vocation, will have an impact on many other people. We never fight only for ourselves, and we never fight alone. Our Virgin Mother Mary and the saints we invoke are all helping us with their prayers.

THE LITURGY OF THE HOURS AND THE EUCHARIST

Every priest has the obligation—and every Christian has the invitation—to recite daily the Liturgy of the Hours, whether in community or in private. This requires an even more radical stretching of the priest's interest and love, since the Church prays with Christ for all mankind. The larger part of the Liturgy of the Hours consists of the psalms, which include the widest range of human emotions, expressing attitudes of humble worship, exuberant praise, acute guilt, deadly fear, and trusting or desperate cries for help, as well as exultant gratitude for being rescued from sin, illness, and death. Since Jesus has come to identify with every man of every time, He has adopted the psalms as His own prayer and includes in them, purified and uplifted, all the intentions of mankind. In reciting the Liturgy of the Hours, priests and religious give voice to this universal prayer of the Church. Obviously, we cannot feel the emotion of every psalm when we pray, but with our will we can embrace all the intentions expressed in them.

Since the official prayer of the Church centers on, and derives from, the Eucharist, the celebration of the Eucharist should also be the center of the priest's personal prayer life. By offering the gifts of bread and wine, the priest intends to offer the whole Church; this includes those who "take part in this offering", "those who seek [God] with a sincere heart", all of human work, and even the whole material universe. The Father does not reject our material offerings, nor the intentions expressed through them; rather, He takes seriously our desire (inspired by His grace) to offer Him a pleasing and perfect sacrifice of atonement, thanksgiving, and praise. Just as the gifts of bread and wine are changed into the sacrificed and risen humanity of the Son, so too are our offerings of ourselves, our work, and all creation united with, and transformed into, the Son's perfect gift of self. We often forget that the center of the Eucharist is not our own gift, but the sacrifice of Christ Himself. And if we suffer from inadequacy as we try to embrace the personal disposition of Christ in His sacrifice, we can always ask for

Mary's help. Being full of grace, Mary alone fully accepted and offered the sacrifice of her Son when she uttered her Yes at the Annunciation and again most especially at the foot of the Cross. Because Mary has been given to us as our mother in the order of grace, she is anxious to help us in the celebration of the Eucharist.

MEDITATION

If we do not develop a personal prayer life, our celebration of the Eucharist and our recitation of the Liturgy of the Hours may easily become a mindless routine or, at best, a tedious obligation. Growth in the spiritual life demands some form of daily meditation in which, instead of mono-loguing to God, we begin to listen to Him. There are many different approaches to a successful meditation. Each one of us should adopt a way that personally suits him best. Here I will present only some general guidelines.

The goal of meditation is to develop sensitivity to God's presence. Even though most of the time we do not feel it, our faith teaches us that He is always there: not even a sparrow falls to the ground without His knowledge and will. God constantly sends us coded messages, so to speak, not through extraordinary, earth-shaking interventions, but through the normal flow of events. Yet only a sensitive heart can decode the ciphers. As the Jewish philosopher Martin Buber observes, all that happens, even the simple flow of events, is a call addressed to me. True faith begins when I become aware that everything that happens has a message for me, when I suddenly realize that a presence confronts me.

One prerequisite for Christian meditation is the belief that God works "mighty deeds" in our own lives similar to those He worked in the history of Israel, Jesus, and the Church. As I said before, what Christ once did visibly, He does every day spiritually in the lives of the faithful. If we become convinced of this, we will read the Bible not merely as a source of information but also as God's Word spoken to us here and now. This Word is as almighty today as it was yesterday. If we have faith, this Word will raise us from the dead, restore our sight, or straighten our paralyzed limbs so that we may walk in His way.

1. The Process of Meditation

The most important preparation is *presence to ourselves*. We should not try to escape from ourselves by pumping up some lofty religious emotions. God waits for us inside our real selves, not in some imaginary, idealized self. We should admit our poverty—all those feelings, resentments, envies, and cravings that we are ashamed of and yet that are part of ourselves. God hears only an honest prayer, the cry from the depth of our misery.

Once we have gotten in touch with our true selves, we can clear some *silence* and *hunger* in our hearts. A story about one of the Desert Fathers may help here. A young man came one day to an old spiritual father and implored him, "Father, teach me how to find God." The old man did not reply but started toward the river nearby. Surprised, the young man followed him in silence. When they arrived at the river bank, the old hermit grabbed the youth, dunked him, held him under water until he almost drowned, and then finally pulled him back above the surface, gasping. "What did you desire most while you were under water?" asked the hermit after he had let the young man catch his breath. "Air, of course", he replied. The old man responded, "If you desire God so passionately as you were craving air while you were under the water, you will find Him." If we have this desire for God, we should be confident. Our desire for Him is a sure sign that He wants to be found by us. We could not desire God if His grace was not already at work within us.

The next step is to *read* a passage from the Bible (or from a good spiritual book) *slowly* and *peacefully*, pondering, almost tasting, each word. I might also imagine a scene from the life of Jesus and identify myself with one of the characters: depending on my changing needs, sometimes I am the disciple whom Jesus encourages or reprimands, the sinful woman to whom He says, "Neither do I condemn you; go, and do not sin again" (Jn 8:11), or perhaps the self-righteous Pharisee whom Jesus tries to shake out of his complacency. We should allow the words of Jesus to sink in, to make an impact on our mind and heart. Sometimes we will find what we need immediately, but sometimes we must continue reading longer until some words strike us.

Then let us ask, *"Lord, what do you want me to do?"* For instance, if I am thinking about the words of Jesus, "Blessed are the peacemakers", I could examine what prevents me from being at peace and spreading peace. What is the cause of my restlessness? What are those situations where my peace could influence others? Then I could ask: What is the secret of Jesus' peace and how is it different from the peace of this world? How can it coexist with struggle and suffering? I could beg Jesus with full trust to give me a share in His peace, knowing that He inspired this request in me so that He might also grant it to me. The Word is living and active, and each prayer should strive to let it penetrate more into our everyday lives.

Finally, let us *thank God for what we received*—even if we feel that we did not receive anything. It is important

that we meditate every day about twenty to thirty minutes
regardless of our mood. We will see only later that it was
worth the effort. Even if our heart and mind remain empty
and dry during the meditation, it may still make us more
sensitive to God's signals during the day. This means that
we perceive a harsh criticism, a sincere smile, or a beautiful sunset as God's personal gifts to us. God remains quite
unpredictable: He takes the initiative when and how He
wants. But without personally striving every day to keep
our ears open, we may not hear God when He decides
to speak.

2. When to Meditate?

The opportune time for meditation depends on individual needs. For some, the best time is in the early morning
before the daily chores and duties have drained them of all
energy. Some, however, cannot keep their eyes open or
their minds going at an early hour, and for them, the ideal
time might be in the evening, when they are alone, at peace,
and still wide awake. For me, the best way is to divide the
time for meditation between evening and morning. I read
the text once at night and think about it peacefully before
I fall asleep. When I awake in the morning, I return to it
and pray with it. After such a conscious and subconscious
preparation, the words of Scripture will sink in much more
effectively than after one cursory reading in the morning.

3. Material for Meditation

God's Word, which enlightens and changes our hearts,
can be found most reliably in the biblical Word of God.
The Bible, then, is the most important spiritual reading, to
which we should return time and again, even if sometimes
other books of spirituality or lives of the saints help make

the words of the Bible come alive and speak to us more effectively. There are different ways of choosing scriptural material for meditation. If I have a specific problem or question (for instance, "What is the meaning of this crisis I have to endure?" or "How can I pray better?"), I could try to find some Bible passages that promise an answer to my question. Several Bible editions, such as the Jerusalem Bible, have a topical index that can help us find the texts we are looking for. When we do not have any particular question or problem, we may want to use the readings of the Mass for the day or read through a whole book of the Bible little by little over a longer period of time, selecting a passage for each day.

4. *Centering Prayer?*

As dialogue with the Hindu and Buddhist forms of meditation multiplied in our age, a trend developed within Catholicism that regarded the work of the imagination and discursive reasoning as suitable only for beginners. Those who found these methods unhelpful were encouraged to empty their minds of images and concepts and, by the silent and slow repetition of a word, prepare themselves to sink into a deeper level of consciousness, into "centering prayer" where they could find God present in their souls.

The Trappist fathers Thomas Keating and Basil Pennington,[2] as well as the Benedictine John Main,[3] find this kind of non-discursive prayer well attested in the patristic age and in the teachings of the great Spanish mystics Saints

---

[2] See M. Basil Pennington, *Centering Prayer: Renewing an Ancient Christian Prayer Form* (Garden City: Doubleday, 1980); Thomas Keating et al., *Finding Grace at the Center* (Still River: St. Bede Publications, 1978).

[3] *Christian Meditation: The Gethsemane Talks*, 4th ed. (Tucson: Medio-Media, 2001).

Teresa of Avila and John of the Cross. Catholic advocates of centering prayer make it very clear that the technique of emptying the mind while repeating slowly and silently a short word, a kind of mantra, like "love" or "Jesus" or "*Marana-tha*", does not automatically produce a mystical experience but rather prepares the person for God's grace, which comes on the Lord's own terms, as a free gift. Teresa and John insist that "the prayer of quiet" (which this movement claims to revive) will be given by God to people at the time determined by God alone.

The beneficial effects of centering prayer in some people cannot be reasonably denied. Still, there are risks. The technique of readying oneself to slip into a non-discursive consciousness can turn into an attempt to manipulate the soul into a deeper awareness of God's loving presence. God, however, does not respond to manipulation, and thus a meditator may wind up captivated simply by the depth of his own consciousness, into which he withdraws seeking peace of mind.

I have not studied centering prayer enough to provide an adequate evaluation. What I know can only be put in conditional sentences. The biblical criteria for discernment are clear: if a spiritual exercise produces good fruits, the fruits of the Spirit ("love, joy, peace, patience, kindness, goodness, faithfulness, gentleness, self-control"— Gal 5:22–23), then the Spirit of God is truly active in the prayer of that soul. But those who fall in love with centering prayer to the point of devaluing the Eucharist and other liturgical prayers, or to the point of losing interest in the mysteries of Christ the man, His birth, life, Passion, and Resurrection, are being led by their own consciousness rather than by the Holy Spirit. The human soul has an enormous hidden potential, and its activation through centering prayer can charm the soul with its own beauty and power. If, however, God's Spirit is truly active in the contemplation, the one praying will be more eager to participate in the Eucharist, the Liturgy of the Hours, and the contemplation of Scripture. Centering prayer should spur them to turn with even greater desire to appropriating and tasting the biblical Word, as the great contemplative saints have always done.[4]

ADORATION BEFORE THE BLESSED SACRAMENT

After a short eclipse resulting from a faulty interpretation of Vatican II, adoration of the Blessed Sacrament has made a powerful comeback.[5] Wherever it has been reintroduced in any significant way—whether in parishes or in religious communities—it has proven abundantly fruitful.[6] The prayer lives of both pastors and flocks have deepened; parish communities have become more prayerful and more united; priestly vocations have budded. Adoration bears fruit in priests and laity alike.

Many have objected that worship of the Blessed Sacrament is a late medieval practice that replaced frequent Communion and therefore was an unhealthy development. This, however, is a dangerous half-truth. Adoration should not replace Holy Communion. On the other hand,

[4] See Congregation of the Doctrine of the Faith, "Letter to the Bishops of the Catholic Church on Some Aspects of Christian Meditation", October 15, 1989, which directly addresses the question of how Eastern methods of meditation should and should not be integrated into Christian prayer.

[5] This section on adoration has been adapted from my *Wedding Feast of the Lamb: Eucharistic Theology from a Historical, Biblical and Systematic Perspective* (Chicago: Hillenbrand Books, 2004), pp. 225–29.

[6] The situation of the Eastern-rite Catholic Churches and Orthodox churches is different. Their Eucharistic liturgies are much longer than ours and there are more opportunities for adoration within the Eucharistic celebration itself.

without the practice of adoration outside the Mass, the celebration of the Eucharist and the reception of Holy Communion will easily become a hasty routine or degenerate into a self-celebration of the community. Although the conciliar document on the liturgy, *Sacrosanctum concilium*, does not mention the adoration of the Blessed Sacrament outside of Mass, both the encyclical *Mysterium fidei* of Paul VI and the *Instruction of the Congregation of Rites* insist on its importance, explaining that worshipping the Eucharist outside of Mass has as "its origin and goal" the celebration of the Mass.[7] To assess the significance of adoration, we need to start from this fact: as long as the empirical signs of bread and wine remain, the Eucharistic Lord remains after the Mass in the same state in which He became present at Consecration, the state of self-surrender to the Father and of being nourishing food for us. Jesus wants to remain with us in this form, which He acquired through His Crucifixion and eternalized through His glorious Resurrection throughout all time, from the present until the consummation of history. The lasting presence of the Eucharistic Lord in our churches is the most eloquent form of God's becoming *Emmanuel*, that is, "God with us".[8]

One may object here that the risen Christ is already permanently present in those whom He nourishes in Holy Communion; one might also add that He is by nature omnipresent since He is God.[9] But according to the

---

[7] *Mysterium fidei* (1965); *Instructio de cultu mysterii eucharistici* (1967), 3e.

[8] Matthew emphasizes this mystery by using the literary device of inclusion. See 1:23 and 28:20.

[9] This issue was clarified in Catholic theology at the time of the Catholic-Lutheran controversy about the omnipresence of Christ's humanity. Luther could affirm this omnipresence because of his somewhat monophysitic Christology, according to which the humanity of the risen Christ takes on the attributes of divinity.

biblical evidence, the risen Christ remains a true human being, and therefore, He cannot be ubiquitously present in His humanity. He is indeed present in all those who believe in Him and love Him, but only to the extent that they allow Him to be present through their love and faith. No Christian has ever been or will ever be substantially and totally Jesus Christ. It is only in the form of food and drink that He is permanently, totally, substantially present in His own crucified and risen humanity. The eucharistic presence of Christ fulfills and even surpasses the perennial desire of mankind for a sacred place in this universe, a point of permanent contact with the sacred. The Eucharist is that concentrated divine presence which makes God's extended presence perceptible in all creation. It fulfills and surpasses as well the desire of Israel to have the *kabod Yahweh*, the glory of God, dwell in their midst. God's glory can no longer abandon His eschatological temple, nor can He allow His temple to be destroyed, since He forever dwells in Jesus, the new Israel.

Of course, Jesus is not a "prisoner of the tabernacle": His being present there does not in any way impede His being present in other places and His working in human hearts. His becoming present through Consecration changes the bread and wine, not Him. To say that Jesus dwells in heaven in addition to the tabernacle is misleading, since this implies that heaven is another place analogous to the space of the tabernacle. Heaven is God's transcendent realm that penetrates our world and is present in the most intense way where the risen Christ is present in His humanity, inseparable from the Father and the Holy Spirit and from His heavenly court of angels and saints. Thus, we should rather say that the tabernacle is heaven itself present among us. It is the mysterious ladder Jacob saw in his dream, a ladder that joins together heaven and earth. This

ladder, however, is no material object but the person of
the risen Christ Who draws all to Himself (Jn 1:51; 12:32).

Jesus spoke of this profound truth when He said, "I go
away, and I will come to you" (Jn 14:28). His return to
the Father, His transcendent form of glorified existence
at the Father's right hand, enables Him to adopt a new
form of immanence among us. His exaltation results in a
new descent, lowlier and more humble than even the Incarnation itself: the glory of the risen Christ reveals itself in
the new depth of His humility, in a sense even surpassing
His humiliation on the Cross. In order to be completely
available for entering into us and feeding us, Christ lowers Himself to the level of "things"; he "becomes" bread
and wine, the only purpose of which is to provide nourishment and joy to human beings. The Son of God thus
reveals His divine transcendence not in His splendid isolation from us, but in overcoming even the last remaining
distance and separation between Him and His creatures,
while respecting our freedom and appealing to our love
rather than coercing us by fear. Ironically enough, some
Catholic theologians insist that since Christ is present as
food in the Eucharist, He should not be worshipped but
eaten. Yet precisely *because* He has become as low and
insignificant as ordinary food and drink for our sake, He
deserves our worship and gratitude.

The tension between Christ's humble form of appearance and His glorious existence in heaven determines our
relationship to Him in the Eucharist. When we are present
before Him in the Holy Eucharist, we are in the presence
of heaven itself: the joy of the risen Christ rescales our
sense of the sufferings and tragedies in our world, giving us
a foretaste of the ultimate triumph of love and granting
us insights and energy to comfort others. As Blessed Charles
de Foucauld, the great worshipper of the eucharistic Christ
in the deserts of Africa, is once said to have asked, "How

can I be sad when my beloved is already in the joy of his Father?" On the other hand, His humble form of presence reassures us of His ability and willingness to make our sufferings His own in a way that surpasses all understanding. From Saint Paul—who wanted to fill up in his own body what is lacking in the sufferings of Christ—to Origen, to Gregory of Nazianzus, to Pascal, and even to the saints of our age, Christian mystics have been aware that the fullness of joy in the risen Christ coexists with His agony in His members up to the end of the world. This means that the risen Christ extends Himself into the very being of the worshipper, prays and suffers through him, with him, and in him. In this way Christ turns our life and sufferings into a well-pleasing sacrifice to His Father. Thus, a mysterious exchange takes place between the worshipper and Christ. Christ makes our sufferings His own and gives us a share in His joy. The priest needs time, time spent in adoration before the Eucharist, in order to become more aware of the incredible mystery of this exchange. In such communing with Christ by desire, the priest will develop a much greater sensitivity for celebrating the Eucharist with awe and joy.

INTERCESSORY PRAYER

In all his prayers, the priest appears before Christ charged with responsibility for all the faithful entrusted to his care. Paul tells his readers at the beginning of most of his letters that he gives thanks for them constantly, and he reminds them of his deep communion with them. His words apply to priests in a special way: "If we are afflicted, it is for your comfort and salvation; and if we are comforted, it is for your comfort, which you experience when you patiently endure the same sufferings that we suffer" (2 Cor 1:6). So a priest's prayers, even those that center on his most personal problems, affect those entrusted to his care.

When a priest celebrates the sacraments and sacramentals, the efficacy of his prayer does not depend on his personal holiness but on the almighty power of Jesus Christ and the faith of the Church. His intercessory prayers before or outside the adoration of the Blessed Sacrament, on the other hand, depend on his personal standing before the Lord. Yet the grace to become a holy intercessor for his people is available to him in the Sacrament of Holy Orders. Once a priest realizes that God has decided from all eternity to grant certain graces to certain people at the intercession of their priest, he may have more incentive not to tire of praying for his faithful. God loves the prayer of the shepherd for his sheep. If the priest's prayer for a conversion remains fruitless, he should remember the words of Saint John Vianney to one of his fellow priests: "You have done all in your power? Are you so sure of it? Did you fast and give alms?"[10] If a priest cooperates with the grace of his ordination, Origen's metaphor will be realized in him: he will be conformed to what he celebrates—his words, his life, and his person will become nourishing food for his people; or, rather, through *His* words, life, and person, Christ will nourish the faith and love of those whom the priest serves.

Humility and Boldness

The story of a genuine vocation often includes, sooner or later, an "end of the rope" experience. This is the realization

---

[10] Anonymous, *The Life of Saint John Vianney, the Curé of Ars* (New York: Joseph Schaeffer, 1911).

that I simply cannot live up to my call, and that I have no will to continue. Moses cannot go to Pharaoh because he stutters. Jeremiah complains that he is too young to speak. Isaiah is struck with deadly fear on account of his sins. Paul complains about the thorn in his flesh. Peter wants to leave Jesus because the miraculous catch of fish reveals to Peter his own unworthiness. Saint Ignatius of Loyola is tempted to commit suicide in the cave of Manresa because of his sins. God allows us such near-despair moments so that we may learn to depend entirely on Him and thereby open up to His grace. If we persevere in prayer, we will discover with Saint Paul that God's "grace is sufficient" for us, and we may even boast gladly of our "weaknesses, that the power of Christ may rest upon" us (2 Cor 12: 9).

The realization of our total unworthiness and of the almighty power of God's forgiving and transforming grace will lead us at the same time to humility, boldness, and freedom: humility, because without God we are literally nothing; boldness, because with God we can do anything He wants us to do; freedom, because as long as we do what we recognize to be His will, we have nothing to fear, for even our defeats will turn into blessings. According to Saint Bernard, Mary was not only the humblest human being in history but also the boldest.

If a candidate for the priesthood should consider himself connected in his prayers to all his future faithful, how much more the ordained priest? Reading the beginnings of the letters of Saint Paul, we see that he is constantly thinking of his own "children" in prayer. He always gives thanks to God for the graces they have received and prays unceasingly for their progress and final perseverance. Paul can do all this because he longs for them in the *splanchnoi Christou Iesou*, literally, in the guts (often translated as "heart") of Jesus Christ (Phil 1:8). Since Jesus Himself prayed to His

Father that His disciples might share in the very love with
which the Father loves Jesus and with which Jesus loves
the disciples, we not only *can* but *should* ask for this grace.
It is not presumptuous to do so; in fact, it would be a sign
of a lack of faith if we did not dare to ask for it. God will
give us priests the grace to love our people with the very
love and very heart of Jesus Christ, provided that we do
not want to "steal" it for ourselves by attributing this love
to our own efforts. If we truly share in Jesus' love, our
hearts will be stretched wide enough to embrace all those
God entrusts to our care. As Paul said, "our heart is [open]
wide" (2 Cor 6:11). This means that our people are invited
to enter our hearts in order to find in them interest, empathy, help, and protection. If we experience indifference or
aversion toward someone entrusted to our care, we must
beg God to change our heart, and until that change happens, we should at least love that person by our actions.

PRAYER, MISSION, AND REFORM

At the decisive junctures of the Church's history, renewal
has always started with prayer, the prayer of people who
fully surrendered to God and allowed the life-giving energies of the Holy Spirit to work through them. After the
Constantinian alliance of church and state watered down
the general quality of Christian life, the great bishops
Athanasius, Basil, Gregory of Nazianzus, Cyril of Alexandria, and John Chrysostom all learned to pray among the
hermits and monks in the deserts of Egypt and Asia Minor
before ordination. At the time of the barbarian invasions,
the most powerful evangelizing impulse came from a cave
in Subiaco, Italy, where Saint Benedict of Nursia was
immersed in prayer for many years. His monk priests and

bishops Christianized the barbarian tribes of Europe in the following centuries. Bernard of Clairvaux was praying in a roadside chapel in Burgundy when he reached his final decision to enter the new monastery of Cistercium, from which there emerged a renewed monasticism that penetrated and fecundated the Church in the twelfth century. The return to evangelical poverty and charity in the thirteenth century was inspired by the words Francis heard in prayer before the crucifix in the crumbling old chapel of San Damiano in Assisi: "Francis, my church lies in ruins. Build it up." At the time of the Protestant Reformation, the fireball that entered the heart of Philip Neri as he was praying in the catacombs of San Callisto enkindled many conversions in Renaissance Rome. The struggles of Ignatius of Loyola in the cave of Manresa gave birth to the Spiritual Exercises, which renewed and continues to renew hundreds of thousands of Christian lives throughout the world. The great impetus for renewal through the Second Vatican Council came—as Pope John XXIII himself testifies—from a sudden inspiration. Without assiduous prayer, Paul VI could not have managed the great balancing act of implementing Church reform and resisting the destructive forces unleashed after the Council. Through the media, the many faces of John Paul II became a worldwide school of instruction in the different forms of prayer—and its development over the course of a life. The youthful trust and shining joy of the robust athlete, the tortured face of the shepherd suffering with Christ, the immobilized face and drooling lips of the dying old man of God—all these images of John Paul II intimated the source from which this extraordinary pope drew the energy to pour into millions of souls trust, courage, and the desire for an intimate communion with Christ. An impressive number of young people, whom some media

like to call the "the JPII generation", have entered seminaries and novitiates in recent years. If the depth of their
prayer life matches their enthusiasm, then a new spring-
time for the Church may be approaching.

CHAPTER 4

The Life of the Priest

We will now take a glance at the priest's personal life, focusing on three of its foundations: celibacy, community, and poverty.

CELIBACY

Already in the Old Testament there is a connection between worship and abstinence from sexual contact. Israel greatly valued marriage and the procreation of children, but she saw sex as involving man in this world and thus preventing him from being fully consecrated to God. Moses ordered the Israelites to be continent for one day before God would descend on Mount Sinai to proclaim his law. When a priest officiated at the altar in the Temple of Jerusalem, he had to live in a special room, separated from his wife.

As we will soon see, the New Testament provides us with a rich theology of celibacy, incarnate in the examples of Jesus, Paul, and John. Fundamentally, the link between Christian priesthood and continence seems to derive from the application of the Old Testament practice of abstinence while serving at the altar. Yet unlike the priests of the Old Covenant, New Testament priests serve at the altar not just periodically, but continuously throughout their lives. In fact, their entire lives have to be a "spiritual sacrifice", and continence therefore also has to be practiced throughout their lives. Priestly continence or celibacy seems to have started out as a spontaneous custom, but we have evidence that it became obligatory in the Latin Church at least from the fourth century. At that time in the East, only the bishops had to be celibate or continent.[1] Obviously, monks and hermits who withdrew to the deserts of Egypt and the Middle East lived in continence, and after they learned the art of spiritual living, many of them were invited or coaxed into becoming priests or bishops. After this, they began exploring the wealth of scriptural wisdom regarding celibacy.

According to the New Testament and the Fathers, the whole Church—men and women, single and married—is called to become the bride of Christ (2 Cor 11:2; Eph 5:22–33; Rev 21:1–4) by uniting with Him in pure love. Some share in this union with Christ through marriage and others through celibacy. Couples who receive the grace of the Sacrament of Marriage learn to love and serve Jesus Christ through loving and serving one another. Those who are called to celibacy freely renounce sexual relations "for the sake of the kingdom of heaven" (Mt 19:12). They do not by any means despise marriage, but rather want to reserve all their psychic and physical energies to prepare the way for God's reign, the great wedding feast between Christ and mankind. Rather than being bound to one man or woman, they want to unite themselves to Christ directly and help many others enter into union with Him. They know that the full spiritual marriage is between Christ and the Church and between Christ and the individual

---

[1] If married men were ordained bishops, they had to live in sexual continence after ordination.

soul insofar as the individual soul lives the mystery of the Church. This divine-human love is a consuming fire, infinitely stronger than human married love. Marriage on earth draws its own fire from this heavenly marriage, which utterly transcends it. We should not confuse the passion of divine love with the changing ebb and flow of emotions, feelings of high and low. Trust and faith—naked, pure faith—alone can lift us out of ourselves and into communion with God. For those who have received the call to celibacy, the invitation to a more direct participation in the wedding feast of the Lamb, marriage would mean a division of heart (1 Cor 7:33–34) and a restriction. Were they married, they would have to focus their psychic energies on their families before all else. Although this kind of familial love can give compelling witness to Christian self-sacrifice, the vocation of consecrated people is to extend their love to *many* men and women and to present each of them "to Christ ... as a pure bride to her one husband" (2 Cor 11:2).

We might also attempt to understand the mystery of Christian celibacy from another viewpoint: the central role of sexuality in personal communion and communication. Unless perhaps we have obscured its value by promiscuity, we know that sex is meant as an intimate way of communication. In marriage—where sexual relations should develop to their full potential—the gift of one's body to the other can express a radical gift of one's whole self, both body and soul. It is indeed the most dramatic way of being in one another and for one another. The consecrated man senses, often instinctively, that his sexual powers hold the key to a radical way of giving himself. Through his celibacy, he longs to give God his whole self, both soul *and* body. In the words of Saint Paul, "the unmarried woman or virgin is anxious about the affairs of the Lord, how to be holy in body and spirit" (1 Cor 7:34).

The consecrated man is, of course, aware that God is not a sexual being and that no one can reach God through his sexual powers. The Bible condemned from the beginning any form of sacred prostitution, the perverse attempt to reach the sacred through sexual relations. The celibate can do only what Mary did in her virginity: not give away the key to one's own gift of self. With Mary, the consecrated man wants to remain "unfulfilled" and persevere in the attitude of prayer and expectation. He waits for God's initiative. He prays that God may look down on the lowliness of his servant (Lk 1:48) and ignite his soul with the fire of His own love. If God grants this, the energy that would normally be used for loving one's spouse and children is redirected into loving God and all those whom God entrusts to the man's care. For the consecrated man, then, his renunciation of sexual love becomes the form of his gift of self to God and to God's people.

The celibate, however, runs a much greater risk than a married person. If his faith fades and his prayer dries up, he may close in on himself and become in the end incapable of loving either God or man, his humanity withered away in sterile isolation and egotism. Husband and wife, on the other hand, must at least curtail their egotism by sharing their income, their time, and their bed, if they want the marriage to last. A dry season in the life of a consecrated man presents him with a great temptation to wall himself off, to despair of love for God and man, perhaps even to seek worldly power or break his vows. Yet if he keeps trusting and praying, his hope will not be disappointed. Although he may not *feel* any more love than before, he will be able to help those who come to him and help ease the burden of those who themselves suffer from loneliness and despair. His own suffering—of which celibacy is a part—will enable him to understand and accept those who suffer. Still, his cross of celibacy should not be exaggerated.

More often than not, it is no more grueling than the hard-ships of those who have to raise a family.

If the consecrated man's love for Christ and for people is real, he will bear witness to the reality of Jesus, Who is the source of his love and peace. His presence among people will be a reminder that the "future age" is real, since his ability to be human and loving without the natural support of a marriage points to a power greater than his own, the power of God's coming kingdom of love. In the kingdom, there will be no need for sexual relations, since everyone will be united to the risen, spiritual body of Christ and to one another in a virginal communion of body and spirit (Mt 22:30).

Looking at celibacy from this perspective, we should not be surprised that the Church clings to it in spite of great pressure from the world and even from her own ranks. In the Roman rite of the Catholic Church, only men who believe they have received the gift (*charisma*) of celibacy and who commit themselves to a celibate life are ordained to the priesthood. The Church, of course, could change her law on this matter, since it is a discipline, not a dogma. Saint Peter was married, and many bishops and priests were married in the first centuries. Even today, in Eastern Catholic rites, married men may be ordained.[2] Nevertheless, in our times, the Roman Church considers the celibate state freely chosen for the sake of Christ to be so important that she would rather accept a lower number of candidates for the priesthood than change her law.[3]

[2] Married priests from the Episcopal and Anglican Churches, after the necessary preparatory phase of conversion and initiation, may also be ordained Catholic priests.

[3] Even if the Church were eventually to change her requirement of celibacy for the diocesan priesthood, members of religious orders, including priests, would still continue to take a vow of celibacy. It is worth noting that in the Eastern rites where most parish priests are married, people generally prefer the celibate monks to the married clergy when it comes to confession and spiritual guidance.

A survey of Church history reveals a close correlation between the state of the Church and the state of clerical celibacy. For example, after the Church became a legally accepted—and even preferred—society under Constantine the Great, its ranks filled with many people who simply embraced the faith superficially in the hope of some secular advantage; after all, Constantine appointed bishops as judges over their people, dressed them in purple robes, and ranked them with senators. During this same time, however, a great number of Christians, seeking to live as authentic disciples, withdrew to the deserts to pray and to combat the Devil in his "natural habitat", renouncing not only the comforts of the imperial court, but the consolation of a family. In time, some of these celibate hermits and monks became famous for their holiness and wisdom and were invited or pressured to become priests and bishops, with vast spheres of influence. These spiritually mature men, including Saints Basil, Gregory of Nazianzus, and Augustine, gave a spiritual vigor to their office that lax, careerist bishops simply could not. To give another example, after the barbarian invasions left the Roman Empire physically and morally devastated, it was the monks of Saint Benedict of Nursia who had the lion's share of converting, civilizing, and educating the tribes that roamed across Europe. At the beginning of the Middle Ages, when clerical celibacy was to a large extent forgotten or ignored, the Benedictine monks of Cluny founded a thousand dependent priories, and their beautiful liturgy—as well as the many bishops and several popes who came from their ranks—revitalized the spiritual life of both the clergy and the people. When in the twelfth century the spiritual élan of Cluny diminished, the Cistercians, Augustinians, and Norbertines counterbalanced the secularizing tendencies of the bishops who doubled as rich feudal lords. Then as peasants in the thirteenth century migrated to growing cities and found themselves in abject poverty, the Franciscans and the Dominicans sought out these urban poor and showed them the true Church of Christ.

Unfortunately, in the subsequent centuries, the spiritual energies of the European Church ran low, and while there lived many individual saints, no reform movement reached the critical mass needed to prevent the general spiritual decline of Europe—a decline evidenced most famously by the sale of indulgences and the corruption of the Renaissance popes. In this context, the eruption of the Protestant Reformation becomes more understandable. Although there were some reform movements within the Church before Luther's appearance, they gathered impetus and powerful spiritual energy only in the second half of the sixteenth century. The Jesuits of Saint Ignatius of Loyola, the Oratorians of Saint Philip of Neri, and the Discalced Carmelites of Saints Teresa and John of the Cross are only several examples from a large crop of saints and religious orders that promoted the renewal of the post-Reformation Catholic Church. There can be no doubt that their astounding energy and fire were fueled by an intimacy with the Lord, kept vibrant by their commitment to the vow of celibacy.

COMMUNITY

1. Diocesan Priests

Although most diocesan priests do not live in community like religious do, they are immersed in the life of their parish, of their diocese, and of the Church.

On every level of authority in the Church, we find a twofold relationship: pope-bishops, bishop-priests, pastor-faithful. The pope is head of the college of bishops, but he is also a brother to them. The purpose of his headship is to promote communion among the bishops in the unanimity of faith and mutual love. Similarly, the relationship of the bishop to his priests is both paternal and fraternal, as the pastor of a parish is both father and brother to his parishioners. On each level, authority exists for the sake of communion. What the bishop Saint Augustine says about his relationship to his people applies just as well to the pastor's situation in the parish:

> Pray for strength for me as I pray that you may not be a heavy burden for me. For the Lord Jesus would not call the burden his own if he did not carry it with the carrier. But you also support me that, according to the Apostle's injunction, we may carry each other's burden and that in this way we may fulfill the law of Christ. If he does not carry with us, we collapse. What I am for you frightens me, but what I am with you comforts me. For I am bishop for you and I am a Christian with you. The first is the name of the office I assumed; the second the name of the grace I received. The first causes danger, the second leads to salvation. We are tossed about in the vast sea by the storm of action; but recalling in whose commission we are laboring, we enter, as it were, the secure harbor by this calming reflection; laboring on our own tasks we find rest in the common gift. So if it delights me more that I have been redeemed with you than that I am your superior, then, according to the Lord's command, I will be more effectively your servant since I will be not ungrateful for the price by which I merited to be your fellow servant. . . .
>
> Therefore, we ask you also, brothers, and command you, do not receive God's grace in vain. Make fruitful our ministry. You are God's ploughing field: on the outside accept the sower and the irrigator, inside the one who makes you increase. The restless must be warned, the faint-hearted comforted, the weak carried, the

contradicting refuted, the insidious avoided, the ignorant taught, the idle awakened, the quarrelling repressed, the conceited reprimanded, the hopeless uplifted, the litigants pacified, the destitute helped, the oppressed liberated, the good affirmed, the bad tolerated, and all of them loved. Please help us both by your prayer and your obedience in such a great multiplicity of various activities so that we may rejoice not so much in presiding over you but in being helpful for you.[4]

We are moved by the warm, confident tone of Augustine's conversational style. He talks to his people as to his friends, shares with them both his anxieties and his joys. Yet at the same time he calmly asserts his own episcopal authority as his way of being a servant—"We ask you also, brothers, and command you, do not receive God's grace in vain." The Latin text better expresses Augustine's approach: *praecipientes rogamus*, literally "in commanding, we ask you". As their friend he asks them, but as their pastor he commands them. Yes, Augustine is a friend to his people, and at the same time he is also a bold, no-nonsense leader, though one who adapts to the character of each one in his flock. "Servant leadership" for Augustine means neither hard-nosed subordination nor a weak, permissive attitude.

In our own age, the good pastor is, on the one hand, a strong leader, but at the same time, he tries to develop a congenial relationship with everyone in his community. He cannot do everything by himself, so he searches for the gifts (charisms) in his parish, people who are willing and able to shoulder responsibilities. There is a need in most places for liturgical ministers, cantors, organists, and

[4] *Sermo* 340 (translated by author).

youth ministers, as well as a need for those who can care
for the sick and elderly, assist with marriage preparation,
help the divorced, or reach out to individuals interested in
the Church. Still, the pastor must not abandon the principle of one-man oversight. Although he should avoid the
temptation to meddle and control, he should never abdi-
cate final responsibility for any parish activity, no matter
how competent the person in charge is. Indeed, one needs
much more refined leadership qualities to work with many
delegated leaders than to try (unsuccessfully) to do everything by oneself.

The ministry team in a parish is unlike a team in a for-
profit company. Unlike a business, the ministry team's
goal is not to get rich or advance in ranks but to become a
loving family, a model and inspiration to draw increasingly
more people into the arms of the Church. In this sense,
the Holy Family can be an icon for the ideal parish. Just as
Mary and Joseph became an intimate couple by together
loving and raising the Child Jesus, the members of a parish collaborate with each other, not on the basis of kin-
ship, common interest, or mutual attraction, but because
they want to worship and serve Jesus together. There is a
mutual relationship here between the theocentric (God-
centered) and communitarian aspects of parish life. The
more sincerely they love and serve Jesus, the more enthu-
siastically they love and serve one another. Conversely,
strengthening their ties with each other will deepen their
commitment and self-giving to God. Augustine's description of Christian sacrifice as *multi unum corpus in Christo*
("the many as one body in Christ") begins to make sense
only if we realize that our sincere union with each other
is achievable only if we try to give ourselves over to God.

Diocesan priests often struggle with the depressing
experience of loneliness. They work hard all day long to

comfort and uplift people, but when they finally come home, there is no one to uplift them, no one with whom to share their own lives. The temptation might become almost irresistible to channel surf, browse YouTube and Twitter, or engage in other forms of cheap recreation that only leave them more numb and more tired. One false way of alleviating loneliness is to seek out a few compassionate families, becoming attached and expecting to be treated as a family member or, worse, as royalty. Another ersatz solution for priests is to surround themselves with a cohort of fans or "groupies", easily found in any parish—people who love to be insiders or confidants of priests, or perhaps young people seeking affirmation. Surrounded with such a group of flattering lackeys, the priest might think that the parish loves him, while in reality he may only be fomenting the majority's resentment against him and his circle of favorites.

There are more helpful ways of coping with loneliness. The priest might cultivate some hobby like playing the guitar or another instrument, or pick out an exciting and worthwhile book to read at the end of the day. The real remedy against loneliness, however, is a sincere love of prayer. Priests belong to Christ and they need to keep alive and deepen their relationship with Him. Jesus does not magically fill the void or remove the pain. Priests instead must face the void, embrace it, and endure it out of love for Jesus, Who Himself cried out in bitter loneliness, "My God, my God, why have you forsaken me?" Then the hollow will be transformed into a source of compassion and consolation, which they can then give to other lonely sufferers. Love, nourished by Christ through the emptiness and pain of isolation, will break through the narrow circle of admirers and reach out to the forgotten and marginal people, to the poor, the sick, and the dying.

Even though friendship with Christ should be one's main source of strength, no human life is complete without friendship. We have many ways of flourishing without sexual activity, but we cannot flourish without genuine friendships. While there are lay people who could be true friends for the priest, a priestly community is indispensable for a happy priestly life, even if it consists of just two or three priest friends. Only a priest can truly understand another priest. Wherever priests come together regularly for common prayer, Bible study, conversation, and recreation, their priestly work is invigorated, and they become both more confident and more capable of building genuine human relations.

We know—from Paul and many other saints—that Christians, priests especially, are supposed to love people *in God*. Yet for a long time I felt uneasy about this recommendation. It seemed opposed to loving a person for his own sake. If I love someone for God's sake, my thinking went, I am using that person as a means for strengthening my love for God, and therefore not loving that person for his unique self. Every human being is unique, irreplaceable, and mysterious. All description of a person amounts to nothing more than approximation. Viktor Frankl, the famous Austrian psychiatrist and Holocaust survivor, offers a mental experiment to show that what makes someone this or that unique person is beyond any conceptual definition. Suppose you claim to be deeply in love with a woman, but someone makes you an offer. "I will pay you one million dollars if you agree to this exchange: I will give you another girl who will look and sound like your girlfriend, with exactly the same external and internal characteristics. But she will be someone else." Would you accept this trade? If you would, says Frankl, you do not truly love her but have only a passing erotic attraction. Yet if your love is real and deep, no payment is great enough for you to replace your beloved, even with a perfect likeness. The true lover knows his friend's unique identity, which escapes definitions and descriptions. How then can such a personal love, which exists to some extent in every genuine friendship, be reconciled with loving someone in God?

My confusion began to clear up when I finally realized what the phrase actually means. To love someone *in* God means to love that person *as* God loves him, which is possible only if God grants me a share in His own love. God loves His own image in us, yet we are not carbon copies of Him. Each one of us is His unique image, both different from and similar to Him. God's image is what is most uniquely personal in us, and that is our inexpressible mystery. To the extent, then, that I unite myself with God's love, I come close to this deepest level of my friend's personality where he communicates with God, where God incessantly upholds and unfolds the best in him.

Thus, loving people in God and loving what is most personal in them are two sides of the same experience. If my love is united with God's love, I can love people in their profundity, in the unique mystery of their person. If I experience communion with others at that level— provided that my experience is true—it is God's grace that has enabled me to do so. When instead I love others with my own resources alone, I ultimately can reach people only on the surface. I may try to manipulate them by rewards or by gentle persuasion, but even the most refined tactics may be countered with resistance or evasion. Only God's love can reach a person's true depth.

As we contemplate ways to deepen and strengthen the love that joins together pastor and community, a strange saying of Saint Bernard comes to my mind: *Quos amamus, in ipsis profecto requiescimus* ("We find rest in those whom we love"). The word *requiescere* cannot be translated with a single word. It means to find rest, peace, calm, tranquility, and refreshment, all at once. For a long time, I have wondered why Bernard says the opposite of what we normally think: "We find rest, peace, in those who love *us*." If someone is indifferent or even hostile to me, how can I find rest and peace in him? With God's grace I might help him if he is in trouble. But find rest and peace in him? That sounds absurd.

In this *quos amamus* formula, Bernard is in touch with a love infinitely greater than his own heart. This love comes from the heart of God, which the soldier's lance opened up on the Cross at Calvary Hill. If we are bold enough to ask—really ask—to share in this love, we will certainly receive it. Perhaps it will not come immediately; perhaps we need to beg God for a long time, patiently and trustingly. But Jesus Himself gave us the commandment "Love one another as I have loved you." If He commands us to love with His own love, then He will not deny our request to share in it. And in His love we will find rest, peace, assurance, and energy. When someone returns indifference and hostility for our love, it can make us sad, but it cannot take away our peace. We still possess an infinite treasure, a participation in the joyful communion of the Holy Trinity. We sense that the Father's love that reaches us through his Son's heart is patient and long-suffering, at times waiting until a person's last conscious moments before finally breaking through the resistance.

In the same text quoted above, Saint Bernard has prepared another surprise: *Amare in Deo caritatem habere est; studere vero propter Deum amari, caritati servire est.* "To love in God is to possess charity; to strive to be loved for the sake of God is to be at the service of charity." At first reading it might seem odd that such a great ascetic as Saint Bernard deems it virtuous to strive to be loved. Isn't this rather the attitude of a spoiled child? Of course, it depends on why we want to be loved—to be flattered, to gain power, to bask in physical and emotional pleasures. To want to be loved instead for the sake of God, Whose very life is manifest in us, is to want to become what He wants us to become: a loveable masterpiece of His creation, a unique, shining image of His Son the Priest.

2. Priests in a Religious Community

Monastic and semi-monastic communities have their own special challenges. There are, of course, some religious communities whose members more often work alone, such as the Jesuits, and for them, even when there is a common residence, community life does not differ essentially from the life of diocesan priests. While a healthy monastic community provides tremendous support to the individuals, it also calls for a different way of practicing one's priesthood. In a parish where only one or two priests are present, their individual ministries and unique personalities radiate upon the faithful and work as a leaven to form the parish community around them. Where a group of monks live together, however, their witness is primarily communitarian. They rightly insist on remaining together rather than living in different parishes, even when there is a legitimate pastoral need. They may offer weekend assistance at different parishes—unless they are purely contemplative—but otherwise cling to their common prayer and work. At first sight, this attitude might appear narrow-minded and selfish, but upon further reflection, we see that their communitarian way of life serves a genuine pastoral need in its own right. Our people and the world at large need not only individual testimonies about the reality of Christ's

love, but also true Christian communities where the love
of Christ reveals its transforming and creative power. The
world should see how very different individuals, of different age groups, backgrounds, and perhaps ethnicities, are
able to live together, not in a bland tolerance of mutual
coexistence, but rather in active acceptance of and care
for one another, a community that enjoys being together
and in which individual talents develop better than they
could in isolation.

Community life can be greatly helped by celibacy
embraced for the love of Christ. We cannot love Christ
without loving those whom He loves. Even the first hermits in the history of the Church showed their love for
Christ by welcoming guests and sharing with others the
fruits of their labor and their counsels. If we seek Christ,
He will lead us into His community. When the risen Christ
appeared to Saul on the road to Damascus, He told him,
"Rise and enter the city, and you will be told what you are
to do" (Acts 9: 6). The Lord says the same to those whom
He calls today: "Go to the Church, to the seminary, to a
religious community, where you will be told what to do."

Modern man is torn between two contradictory drives.
At times someone might prefer to withdraw from the
oppressive company of others and do "his own thing",
undisturbed by any outside pressure. At other times, the
same person may crave to lose his own fragile identity
in the anonymity of a group, to feel and think *with the
group*. Sometimes gifted individuals end up brainwashed
by a cult or lifestyle that offers them an emotional shelter
at the price of personal identity. A good religious community avoids both extremes, divisive individualism and
mindless group identity. Only a sufficiently strong person
is *free* enough to become a constructive member of a community. He chooses to subject his own interests to those

of the community and accept the community's tasks and commitments as his own. Obedience must be seen in this larger context: the superior assigns the tasks and responsibilities to each member and sees to it that everyone cooperates according to his own ability for the realization of the goals and ideals of the community. Of course, no religious community is a free-floating, independent group, but each is part of the Church and must be dedicated to serving the Church.

In community life, it is easier to develop friendships, loving others in God for their own sake. It may happen, however, that out of fear or resentment, a member chooses the easy, but ultimately disappointing, path of reducing relationships to obligatory community exercises, such as communal prayer or meals, and living otherwise in his own bubble. Well known is the complaint, "I have a hundred brothers but no friend in my community." In community life, we experience again and again the truth of Jesus' words: "Whoever would save his life will lose it; and whoever loses his life for my sake and the gospel's"—we could add "for the sake of his brothers and sisters"—"will save it" (Mk 8:35). In opening up to personal relationships, which involves surrender, we become more alive, more human, and we thereby begin to work more generously for the good of the community. When we give ourselves to a good community, our individual talents and unique potential are not suppressed but rather stretched to the limit. We will be surprised to find that we can do much more and can handle a much greater variety of tasks and jobs than we had ever suspected outside the monastery.

The greatest asset of community life is that we are "mutually encouraged by each other's faith" (Rom 1:12). My faith is rekindled by the faith of my brother, my sagging fidelity by his fidelity. I recognize that the presence of

Christ in my brother's heart makes him strong and hopeful, and so I am inspired to ask Christ for the same grace. By acknowledging the gifts of others—their faith, goodness, and wisdom—and by being grateful for them, I can share in their gifts myself. In this way, I experience what it means that we are all members of the same body.

Perhaps the most serious trials of community life are the moments where I must admit my inability to love my brothers, when my sins and their sins weigh so heavily on me that I begin to lose hope for improvement. At these times, only prayer can help, a prayer from faith, the size of a mustard seed. He who prays this way knows in advance that if he asks for the ability to love his brothers, God will not, in the long run, resist him. Thus, a religious community never becomes a "finished product". It is always both a gift and a task, a present reality and an object of hope. Sometimes it provides a foretaste of our home in heaven; at other times, however, it tastes like an hors d'oeuvre from purgatory.

POVERTY

"We want to be poor with the poor Christ." This was the motto of the first Cistercian monks, but it applies to priests of all times. The Incarnation itself is God's radical act of embracing poverty. The Son Who was rich became poor for us, writes Saint Paul (2 Cor 8:9). The Son emptied Himself of His divine glory, status, and way of life in order to become one of us so that He might share His divine life with us. In His short earthly life, Jesus lived different forms of poverty. At His birth in a stable, Jesus was homeless, lacking any ordinary comfort and material security. Escaping as an infant from His own country, He became a refugee in Egypt. Then during His public ministry, He lived from donations and had "nowhere to lay his head" (Lk 9:58). He ended his life naked, deprived even of his clothes, stretched out upon the most painful and shameful tool of torture: the Cross. Yet during His relatively long "private life" in Nazareth, Jesus earned His living as a carpenter's apprentice and, after Joseph's death, perhaps as a carpenter Himself; such a profession did not mean destitution, but a decent, lower-middle-class existence. Joseph was, in New Testament Greek, a *tekton*, literally a "builder", able to build not only furniture but anything made of wood, including houses and bridges. A few miles from Nazareth there was a booming colonial town, Zippori, which must have provided good job opportunities for Joseph and Jesus. And yet this, too, was a kind of poverty. Priests may be called to live the poverty found in any, or all, of these stages of Jesus' life, and in each of them, they can practice generosity and inner freedom from possessions.

1. Diocesan Priests

Some form of poverty is essential, not only to religious life, but also to the diocesan priesthood. Jesus' words are clear: "If you would be perfect, go, sell what you possess and give to the poor" (Mt 19:21). In these few words, the priest discovers a twofold call with respect to money and material goods.

First, "sell what you possess". Jesus knows that clinging to possessions paralyzes the heart and closes it off to God. Everyone is called to be "poor in spirit"; no one should become a slave of his possessions, but should be generous in sharing with those in need. Without this attitude, no one can enter the kingdom of God. Those whom Jesus calls to the priesthood, however, must do more: give up altogether the desire and effort to accumulate material goods for a life of affluence and luxury. Often, the more a parish priest is appreciated, the more personal donations he receives, and his big temptation becomes the feeling that he has deserved all this and may therefore spend it all for himself, whether on pleasures or on projects. But the Lord calls His disciples to another path.

Renouncing material goods does not mean despising them. To the heart freed from craving, material things reveal what they are: God's gifts, signs of His wisdom, goodness, and beauty. Saint Francis, who never owned an acre of land in his life, enjoyed the blooming meadows of Umbria more than those who actually owned those fields did. Indeed, priests have a right to decent living conditions, in order to be reliable, respectable father figures in their communities. Yet this decency varies drastically across different cultural environments. In a poor country, a well-to-do priest would be a hindrance to, rather than a conduit of, evangelization.

Even priests in comfortable circumstances will likely have to face a kind of radical poverty in old age. At the end of our lives, we should accept that we may lose all independence and even be shipped into a nursing home where we will resemble Jesus during His public ministry. In almost everything, we will depend on others, our space restricted to one half of a small room. We should learn from the example of those priests we know who accepted this extreme poverty and acted out their priestly ministry to those who shared the same nursing home.

Here are a few simple ways in which we priests can discipline our appetite for comfort and for possessions:

- When alone, cook for yourself instead of dining out or ordering. When in a community, accept the food offered at meals, even if you dislike it, rather than creating your own special meal. (Allergies, of course, are a different case.)

- Do not buy a book you need only for a short time, but check it out from the library and return it afterward.
- Do not buy the most expensive cellphone or computer, and do not accumulate gadgets you do not really need. Resist the temptation to alleviate your somber mood by going on a buying spree.

Secondly, Jesus invites the young man to "give to the poor". Besides freeing the heart for God, the renunciation of wealth has another purpose: to help those in need. Here the diocesan priest has an important advantage over the religious. In the case of the latter, the community and its superior decide to what extent he should directly serve the poor. The diocesan priest, on the other hand, is free to be more radically generous with his money. In every time and country in Church history, there have been priests who passed on to the poor all that people gave them. The Church Fathers and the encyclical *Populorum progressio* teach that the priest's goods—beyond what he needs to live and work—truly belong to the poor of his flock. As much as they are able, diocesan priests should, in cooperation with diocesan institutions, tend to the emergency needs of the poor, helping them to find stable employment and a good education for their children.

2. Priests in a Religious Community

But Jesus' counsel to the rich young man did not stop at giving to the poor. There was one further, more crucial step: "And come, follow me" (Mt 19:21). This following is perhaps embodied most visibly in the religious life, whose express *vow* of poverty brings men and women materially closer to the practice of the earliest disciples. Those who followed Jesus during His earthly ministry lived from a common purse. The first Christian community followed their example, with members selling their property and giving the proceeds to the apostles, who distributed to each according to their need (cf. Acts 2:44–46; 4:32–37).

Today, forms of poverty are different in each religious institution, and for many of them, life resembles Jesus' thirty years in Nazareth more than His poverty in birth, public ministry, and death. The living standards of many religious communities today are lower middle class, so to speak. But there are also religious communities that practice various forms of radical poverty even in our times, for example certain Franciscan and Carmelite communities, as well as the Little Brothers and Sisters of Jesus, inspired by Blessed Charles de Foucauld, who lived in northern Africa among the Tuaregs, the poorest of the Saharan poor. By sharing in the poverty of those they serve, these communities create a bond of solidarity. The poor see that a life at the bottom of society can be embraced out of love and lived with joy. Many of these religious communities help to "empower" the poor by making them aware of their personal dignity, their rights, and the ways that they themselves can improve their material, cultural, and spiritual lives.

In all healthy communities, one feature remains constant: religious depend on the community for their material goods. They do not earn anything for themselves, but instead rely on the superior to give or at least permit them what they need, according to their needs rather than their individual earnings. Their sharing of material goods such as common residences, common meals, and community cars, and possibly of common work or projects, promotes brotherhood and family spirit. Naturally, the richer the resources to share, the more likely the flare-ups of emotional tension and irritation in the community, but overcoming these temptations brings about what the Acts of the Apostles says about the early Christian community in Jerusalem: "The company of those who believed were of one heart and soul" (Acts 4:32).

3. Spiritual Poverty

Wealth and poverty do not apply only to money and goods. There are priests and religious who do not crave material goods, but instead cling all the more to their real or imagined intellectual or spiritual superiority, eager to foster their own self-promotion. The following medieval proverb, though clearly an exaggeration, nevertheless contains a grain of truth: *Homo homini lupus, sacerdos sacerdoti lupissimus*—"Man is a wolf to man, but the priest to a priest is the most wolfish of all." The priest has no wife to boost his ego, and if his self-esteem is not firmly rooted in God, he will try to satisfy his human craving for recognition by calling attention to his own real or imagined excellence, perhaps even in the name of ministry or evangelization. He will surround himself with lackeys and flatterers rather than with competent co-workers. To make his image shine brighter, he may gossip about parishioners or fellow priests. In the long run, however, sycophants cannot fill the priest's emotional vacuum, so he might try indulging in food and drink or even engaging in sexual escapades.

There is no way out of such a quagmire other than conversion and a fresh start—a return to spiritual poverty. If a dissatisfied priest turns honestly to the Lord, he will discover at last the true joys of priestly life. He should begin by giving over all that he is, talents and shortcomings alike, with gratitude to God. If he is poisoned by envy, especially toward a fellow priest, let him give thanks to God for the gifts of this other person, turning the poison into a balm. If he is sick with pride, let him develop a sober appreciation, not only for his own talents, but for his weaknesses. Faults, flaws, evil inclinations—the more shameful they are, the better medicine they prove to be when accepted with trust. Moses' stammering tongue led him to rely entirely on God for the success of his mission. The hypersensitive nature of the young Jeremiah, as well as the thorn in Paul's flesh, served as a providential preparation for God's grace to empower human weakness. When man recognizes his own empty-handedness before the Lord, his Creator, he flings himself upon the richness of His power and love.

Thus, if the priest lets go of everything else but care for souls, he will be immensely enriched by the joy of those whom he helps to come closer to Christ. If a priest is satisfied with mediocrity, a bare minimum of prayer, and a lackluster approach to his priestly work, he will never find happiness, and he will become an easy target for temptations. We priests should strive every day to fulfill God's plan for our lives one hundred percent. Let us make ours the prayer of Don Bosco: *Da mihi animas, cetera tolle!*— "Give me souls and take all the rest!" Then we will share many great joys because we will discover the manifold work of God in souls, the many different forms of mercy by which God lures back so many lost souls to Himself. We can make some people aware of what God is doing in their lives and what He is asking them to do. We will enjoy getting acquainted with some beautiful souls who are filled with the fruits of the Spirit: "love, joy, peace, patience, kindness, goodness, faithfulness" (Gal 5:22). But we will also have to engage in battles for souls, pray for them and at time fortify our prayer by fasting, begging and fighting God for them. God is rich in mercy, but in a mysterious way He wants us to wrestle with Him to obtain His blessing, as at one time Jacob had to fight with Him all night until daybreak.

Spiritual poverty also takes flesh in our relationships with others. Like the early Christians who lived from a common purse, we are invited to share our spiritual, emotional, and intellectual goods with one another, in gratitude and joy. Here are a few practical suggestions for living with a spirit of joyful poverty in our interactions and friendships, whether in a parish or in a religious community:

- A community is only as strong as the bond that joins them together. In a religious community and in a parish, this is the common call and common striving to love and serve God. The more this supernatural bond means to us, the more reason we find to enjoy each other's company.
- Do not posture before others. We have all seen parties where almost everyone puts on a mask: the happy spouse, father, businessman, devout church-goer, political wizard. You feel that it is not the persons but the masks who are conversing with each other and that when the party is over, they all let out a big sigh of relief. Always be yourself.
- Find something admirable in everyone. They will sense it, and it will open them up to you.
- Be a good listener. The good conversationalist is not the one who talks much but the one who is sincerely interested in what the other is saying or feeling, the one who is able to "tune in" to him.
- Share something of yourself. This is the essence of real communication. It is easier to listen to someone who is genuinely sharing something of himself—an

experience, a story, an observation—rather than trying to impress the listener or compete with him.

- Be ready to be laughed at and to laugh at yourself; at the same time, never laugh at anyone sarcastically or with an attitude of condescension. Funny things happen in every community, and most of us, more or less frequently, behave in a funny way. Never take an arrogant pleasure in another's faults or defects.

- Be your brother's keeper. If you are close to someone, then you can help him by your example and, occasionally, by sharing with him directly your concern about a fault of his.

- When someone or something grates on your nerves, bring the annoyance and the annoyer to God. The Father loves when His children pray for each other, and in this way even our irritations or resentments may turn into a blessing for us and for the cause of our irritation.

- When all else fails, remember the saying of Blessed Aelred: "[In heaven] everyone will love the other as himself and thus enjoy the other's happiness as much as his own. In this way, everyone will possess the happiness of everyone else, and each individual the totality of happiness. There will be no hidden thoughts or hypocritical sentiments there. This is the true friendship which begins here and is consummated there."[5] Our faults and defects are temporary, and our Father will burn them away in purgatory, if not earlier. In heaven we will fully enjoy each other's company.

---

[5] Aelredus Rievallensis, *De amicitia spirituali*, in *Patrologia latina*, edited by J.-P. Migne, vol. 195 (Paris, 1855), col. 689D, bk. II (translation by author).

CHAPTER 5

Baptism, Confirmation, and the Eucharist

BAPTISM

The theology of baptism is unspeakably rich, and as ancient as the Church herself. Rather than attempting to give any comprehensive picture of the mysterious sacrament, I will open our discussion with an excerpt from a masterful reflection by Pope Benedict XVI, which provides a fresh, illuminating perspective on the traditional doctrine:

> The Lord's last words to his disciples on this earth were: "Go therefore and make disciples of all nations, baptizing them in the name of the Father and of the Son and of the Holy Spirit" (cf. Mt 28:19)....
>
> The choice of the word "*in* the name of the Father" in the Greek text is very important: the Lord says "*eis*" and not "*en*", that is, not "*in* the name" of the Trinity—as when we say that a vice-prefect speaks "on behalf" of the prefect, an ambassador speaks "on behalf" of the government: no. It says: "*eis to onoma*", that is, an immersion in the name of the Trinity, a being inserted in the name of the Trinity, an interpenetration of being in God and of our being, a being immersed in God the Trinity, Father, Son and Holy Spirit; just as it is in marriage, for example. Two people become one flesh, they become a new and unique reality with a new and unique name....

Becoming Christians, in a certain sense is *passive*; I do not make myself Christian but God makes me his man, God takes me in hand and puts my life in a new dimension. Likewise I do not make myself live but life is given to me; I am not born because I have made myself a human being, but I am born because I have been granted to be human. Therefore my Christian being has also been granted to me, it is in the *passive* for me, which becomes *active* in our, in my life. And this fact of being in the passive, of not making ourselves Christian but of being made Christian by God, already to some extent involves the mystery of the Cross: only by dying to my selfishness, by coming out of myself, can I be Christian....

Naturally, being immersed in God I am of course united to my brothers and sisters, because all the others are in God and if I am taken out of my isolation, if I am immersed in God, I am immersed in communion with the others....

To be baptized is never a solitary act by "me"; it is always, necessarily, being united with all the others, being in unity and solidarity with the whole Body of Christ, with the whole community of his brothers and sisters. This event which is Baptism inserts me in community, breaks my isolation. We must bear this in mind in our being Christian.[1]

1. Preparation for Baptism

The rite of baptism differs for children and adults, but it always requires preparation. Adults are normally baptized at the end of the process of Christian catechesis and initiation, typically receiving confirmation and full participation in the Holy Eucharist as well. Infants and minors are baptized, instead, with the faithful assent of their parents

---

[1] Benedict XVI, Lectio Divina at the Ecclesial Convention of the Diocese of Rome (June 11, 2012).

and godparents, who also must be sufficiently prepared. Children should be baptized only if there is a reasonable hope for their Catholic Christian education. Priests ought to use the baptism of children as an opportunity to help the parents or guardians to understand or deepen their knowledge of the sacramental life of the Church and, in particular, the meaning of their child's baptism. We should explain the parents' role in religious and moral education at the different stages of the child's development. In the case of practicing Catholics, one session might be sufficient, but for those who are ignorant of Catholic faith and doctrine, several meetings are in order.

2. Understanding the Doctrine of Original Sin

Instead of providing a detailed itinerary for pre-baptismal instruction, I will focus only on the often-misunderstood doctrine of original sin. Before Vatican II, most Catholic parents looked at baptism as the removal of original sin, imagined as a stain on the soul that would prevent the baby from entering heaven. Today, many parents, detached from this view of the sacrament as a cleansing from sin, believe instead that the essential meaning of baptism is to welcome the baby into the Christian community. Obviously, both views have elements of truth, but each is incomplete by itself.

Original sin is very different from personal sin, for which we are directly responsible before God. Original sin means that, on account of the personal sin of the first human couple, we are born without sanctifying grace; in other words, we are born not as children of God, but only as His creatures, created in His image and likeness. Thus original sin is sin not in the sense of personal culpability, but in the sense of being opposed to God's original plan for man. In the beginning, God intended that our first parents should transmit to their offspring not only natural life but also the supernatural gift of being born as a child of God and an heir to eternal life. After Adam's Fall, the Lord cast him and his family out of the garden and thus out of that spiritual intimacy for which he was created. This was not an injustice on God's part, since being a child of God is a privilege to which no man can lay claim. If we ask why God deprived us of this privilege, we may say with certainty only that He had the right to do so, but there are also some very plausible reasons for His action. God created us as members of one family in which we are closely interconnected both on the natural and supernatural levels. In an ordinary human family, we are born with some inherited conditions—high cholesterol, for example, or mental illness—and often we pass on these weaknesses and diseases to our own children; in a family household, even simple maladies like the cold and the flu can spread like wildfire. So it is with mankind and original sin.

Yet on the supernatural level, men are linked not only on the level of sin but also on that of grace. As Saint Paul writes, "For as by one man's disobedience many were made sinners, so by one man's obedience many will be made righteous" (Rom 5:19). The gift of grace through Christ's sacrifice is infinitely more abundant and powerful than the effects of one man's sin. Through the death and Resurrection of Christ, the child—as well as the adult Christian—is offered in baptism the sanctifying grace that our first ancestors lost. He is elevated to the dignity of a child of God, and he becomes a brother of Christ. Sharing in the relationship that Christ has to His Father, the child is loved and protected by the same love the Father lavishes on His only Son. While a person's natural life grows for some years, reaches a plateau, then gradually declines and comes to an end, the divine life of the children of God can continue to grow and unfold until their last conscious moments and then go on in eternity. In a child's baptism, the divine life is planted as a seed whose development and blossoming depends not only on all those who influence the child, especially parents, but on the growing child's own response to grace.

3. A Theology of Infant Baptism

Many people object to children's baptism on the ground that baptism must be a free, mature assent of faith. To respond, we need to consider, first of all, the historical tradition of the Christian Church. In the New Testament, we read that entire households received baptism, which probably included children and infants (Acts 16:15, 33; 18:8; 1 Cor 1:16). We have explicit testimony about child baptism beginning with the end of the second century. The early practice was to baptize a child of Christian parents or guardians who promised to rear the child in a Christian way. The Church never approved of infant baptism at random. This is still our custom today.

But even if this has been the norm in Church history, does that make it right? What justifies infant baptism? We will make three points. To begin with, the first theological principle we receive from revelation is the absolute priority of God's love to any human response. "Before I formed you in the womb I knew you, and before you were born I consecrated you", says the Lord to the prophet Jeremiah (Jer 1:5). God creates each person in a love beyond all telling, before the child is even aware of his own existence. The relationship between a mother and an infant can help illustrate this dynamic. A mother shows love to her child before he can respond; it is the mother's first loving smile that then inspires the response of the newborn child, bringing him to smile. How much more profoundly, then, does God do this for man? "Can a woman forget her sucking child, that she should have no compassion on the son of her womb? Even these may forget, yet I will never forget you" (Is 49:15). God calls us into being and into the life of the Holy Trinity without our consent or decision. Infant baptism is Christ's embrace of a child, a tangible sign of God's love that will call for personal acceptance gradually, according to the child's growing maturity.

Another point is that God intends to save us not in isolation but in community, mutually dependent on each other. We are as responsible for one another on the supernatural level as on the natural. In fact, the supernatural communion we all have in Christ enables us even to "substitute" ourselves for one another, to "represent" one another. Much as Christ stood in our place to obtain forgiveness for all of us, so we can stand in for the other before God, carrying his burdens. The child's godparents and guardians accept such a radical responsibility. He is baptized in the faith of the Church, represented by those who offer him into the Church.

Thirdly, since Christianity is not an abstract list of truths but life itself—a share in the communion of the Holy Trinity—one must live and experience it in order to appreciate its reality. A professor of theology may be renowned across the world, but if he has never practiced what he teaches, he cannot communicate its reality. He cannot hand on what he has not experienced. Thus, an unbaptized child, who is excluded from participation in the sacramental life of the Church, does not really know Christianity, even if he studies it. If later in life an unbaptized child rejects Christianity because of what he thinks is a mature personal decision, he rejects it unaware of its real value, because he has never truly known it. Christian parents who postpone the baptism of their infants because they do not want force them into the Church, which they see as coercion, in fact act most unjustly. They deny their children the opportunity to experience the fullness of the faith—an intimate knowledge that alone could equip a person to choose or reject the faith in freedom.

4. The Unbaptized

What about those people—most on earth, in fact—who never receive baptism? Pope Benedict XVI speaks lucidly about the destiny of unbaptized pagans, drawing from the vision of Saint Augustine:

> The great Father of the Church [Augustine] introduces a surprising and very timely note: he knows that there are also people among the inhabitants of Babylon who are committed to peace and to the good of the community, although they do not share the biblical faith; the hope of the Eternal City to which we aspire is unknown to them. Within them they have a spark of desire for the unknown, for the greater, for the transcendent: for true redemption.
>
> And Augustine says that even among the persecutors, among the non-believers, there are people who possess this spark, with a sort of faith or hope, as far as is possible for them in the circumstances in which they live. With this faith, even in an unknown reality, they are truly on their way towards the true Jerusalem, towards Christ.
>
> And with this openness of hope, Augustine also warns the "Babylonians"—as he calls them—those who do not know Christ or even God and yet desire the unknown, the eternal, and he warns us too, not to focus merely on the material things of the present but to persevere on the journey to God. It is also only with this greater hope that we will be able to transform this world in the right way. St Augustine says so in these words: "If we are

citizens of Jerusalem ... and must live in this land, in the confusion of this world and in this Babylon where we do not dwell as citizens but are held prisoner, then we should not just sing what the psalm says but we should also live it: something that is done with a profound, heartfelt aspiration, a full and religious yearning for the eternal city."

And he adds with regard to the "earthly city called Babylon," that it "has in it people who, prompted by love for it, work to guarantee it peace—temporal peace—nourishing in their hearts no other hope, indeed, by placing in this one all their joy, without any other intention. And we see them making every effort to be useful to earthly society.

"Now, if they strive to do these tasks with a pure conscience, God, having predestined them to be citizens of Jerusalem, will not let them perish within Babylon: this is on condition, however, that while living in Babylon, they do not thirst for ambition, short-lived magnificence or vexing arrogance.... He sees their enslavement and will show them that other city for which they must truly long and towards which they must direct their every effort."[2]

CONFIRMATION

In the Latin Church, there is much diversity in interpreting the meaning of the Sacrament of Confirmation, with many different opinions on when it should be administered, but it all ultimately rests on one common tradition. We know that in the Apostolic Church and in the Church of the Fathers, confirmation was, as Ambrose writes, the "perfection" or completion of baptism to be administered by an apostle or, later, by a bishop.[3] With the increase of

---

[2] Benedict XVI, General Audience (November 30, 2005) (quoting *In Psalmum* 136:1–2).

[3] St. Ambrose of Milan, *On the Sacraments*, III.II.8 (*PL* 16:434A).

the Catholic population, however, the bishop could not possibly be present at all the baptisms in his diocese, so he therefore offered confirmation to groups of already-baptized Christians gathered from several local churches. With infant baptism becoming the norm, there arose the custom of administering confirmation at a later age, when the children were old enough to understand and appreciate it. Yet confirmation as we understand it today is more than just a renewal or commemoration of baptism. In this sacrament, one receives the seal of the Holy Spirit, and of the Church. What does this really mean? How can we help adolescents and adults to prepare for it? Rather than offering any kind of program for catechesis, I will unpack a few commonly misunderstood principles that will lay the groundwork for a good preparation.

1. Receiving the Holy Spirit

First, before looking at the sacrament itself, we have to consider Who the Holy Spirit is. Candidates for confirmation can only understand the effects of the sacrament in their own hearts to the extent that they open up to this Spirit and know something of His manifold ways, beginning in creation, continued in the history of Israel, fully revealed and communicated by the risen Christ, and present in the life of the Church. The Spirit, in the form of a wind hovering over the chaotic, newly created earth, brought forth life and filled the world with plants and living creatures; then God breathed the spirit of life into man to create him as His images and stewards in the world. The Spirit was given to Moses and shared by the seventy elders who helped him in his governance. The judges before the time of the monarchy—Gideon, Samson, and others—were enabled by the Spirit to rule in Israel and save her

from her enemies. The Spirit inspired the prophets to proclaim the coming of the Messiah, and to announce the
outpouring of this same Spirit upon all mankind at the end
of time (Is 11:1–2; 61:1; Ezek 36:25–27; Joel 3).

In the New Testament, this promise of a full and permanent outpouring of the Spirit is fulfilled in Jesus. He
is conceived by the Holy Spirit in the womb of the Virgin Mary. He hears the Father's words as the Holy Spirit
descends upon Him in the Jordan River. Jesus' public
ministry is directed by the Father, Who communicates
with Him in the Holy Spirit. Jesus is led into the desert by
the Spirit (Mk 1:12), Who then leads Him to Galilee (Lk
4:14). Jesus drives out demons by the Spirit of God (Mt
12:28); He gives thanks to the Father rejoicing in the Holy
Spirit (Lk 10:21). Jesus promises the Holy Spirit to those
who believe in Him (Jn 7:37–39). In the Farewell Discourse in the Gospel of John (13–17), we learn that after
His death, the risen Jesus Himself will come back to the
apostles in the Holy Spirit and will lead them into the truth
of what Jesus told them.[4] Jesus hands over the Spirit both
to the Father and to us as He breathes His last on the Cross
(Jn 19:30), and according to the Letter to the Hebrews, He
offers Himself to God in sacrifice by the eternal Spirit (Heb
9:14). The risen Lord returns to His disciples and remains
with them in the Holy Spirit (Jn 14:15–29). Following His
Resurrection, Christ breathes upon the disciples His Holy
Spirit, Who will make effective their mission of proclaiming the good news (Jn 20:19–23).

The Holy Spirit continues to descend upon Christians
after Jesus' Ascension. We see the amazing transforming
effect of the Spirit on the Apostles at Pentecost and in the

---

[4] For the effects of confirmation, see also *Catechism of the Catholic Church*,
no. 1302.

many gifts manifest in the life of the early Church (Acts 2–5). The Holy Spirit stirs up "love, joy, peace, patience, kindness, goodness, faithfulness, gentleness, self-control" (Gal 5:22–23). Acts 8:14–17 shows us a distinct moment where the Spirit is conferred by the hands of the apostles, and this seems to mark the beginnings of the Sacrament of Confirmation. Philip, one of the seven helpers elected by the community (Acts 6:1–7), had baptized men and women in Samaria, but since he was not an apostle, he could not "lay hands" on the Christians he had baptized, and Peter and John were sent for this purpose.

As we prepare our faithful for confirmation, we should search with them for as many contemporary examples as we can find of the operation of the Holy Spirit in the Church. For example, we can ask them if they have encountered Christians who speak about the mysteries of faith with the power of direct experience. We can also ask them to find signs of the many ordinary charisms in today's Christian communities (joy, peace, eagerness to serve, generosity, care for the sick and elderly, ability to comfort) and tell them about the extraordinary gifts in some of the saints. In this way, we can sensitize them to perceive the signs of the Spirit's work in their own lives.

2. Perfecting the Grace of Baptism

We can say with Saint Ambrose that the grace of confirmation *perfects* the grace of baptism. Just as baptism enables the Christian to live as a child of God both in the liturgy and in daily life, confirmation strengthens the Christian to live as a spiritual adult, working not only for his own salvation but also for that of others, "boldly confessing his faith", as Saint Thomas Aquinas says, and defending it against its enemies. It gives Christians the fullness of the

Holy Spirit, makes them full members of the Church, and enables them to grow into mature believers who by their lives and actions bear witness to Jesus Christ.[5]

During the Church's rite of confirmation, the sacramental sign—the anointing with chrism on the forehead and the simultaneous laying on of hands by the bishop—occurs in unison with the words, "N., receive the gift of the Holy Spirit." Here, the confirmand encounters at once the sacramental character and the grace of the sacrament. The grace is the receipt of the Spirit. Theologians explain the meaning of this sacramental character with an image from the ancient world: in the Roman Empire, soldiers were branded on their skin with the name of the emperor, to make it obvious to everyone that these men belonged to Caesar. In a similar way, baptism and confirmation together mark one's very being as belonging to Christ and to the Father. The sacramental character of confirmation perfects in the soul the indelible spiritual mark of baptism, a mark that cannot be erased even by grave sins. It is a pledge of God's unconditional fidelity to that person: God will give the confirmed person all the graces he needs to develop as a mature Christian. Even if this person sins, God's commitment remains: as soon as he asks sincerely for forgiveness, God renews His life in him and helps him grow.

How is confirmation connected to the Holy Eucharist? By the time most Christians receive confirmation, they have already begun receiving Communion. If the Eucharist is the greatest of all sacraments because it is the very Body and Blood of the Lord, what can the grace of confirmation add to it? Ultimately, confirmation enables us

[5] Saint Paul calls the entire initiation rite "baptism" since it was administered as one continuous rite. But his reference to baptism as being sealed with the Spirit probably points to the laying on of hands (Eph 1:13; 4:30; 2 Cor 1:21–22).

to receive the Eucharistic Lord more fruitfully. Yes, the gift offered to us at Mass—Jesus Christ in the fullness of His humanity and divinity—is infinite, but our ability to receive Him is limited by our finite human nature, sins, and imperfections. Only the Holy Spirit can widen and deepen our heart, sanctifying it so that we may more effectively receive Christ into our hearts and minds. In addition, the Spirit, through the gift of understanding, helps us better grasp the mystery of the Eucharist and better testify about Him to others.

3. When to Administer Confirmation

In the Eastern rite churches, confirmation is the second moment of a single initiation process for infants, administered after baptism and before Holy Communion, which is given to the baby under the sign of a drop of consecrated wine. In the Latin rite churches, however, we find a variety of arrangements according to country or diocese. There are some regions that follow the Eastern way with one combined rite; others administer it when the child reaches the age of reason (seven or eight years old), before First Communion; others administer it at thirteen or fourteen years old; and some dioceses postpone it until ages sixteen to eighteen.

Those who wait until late adolescence believe that confirmation should be given only to those who have enough maturity to accept it freely, and perhaps they also see an advantage in keeping young people under religious instruction for a longer period, up to the time of confirmation. This solution has two great drawbacks. The first is that these teenagers will not have the grace of the sacrament during the most difficult years of their adolescence, when their inner turmoil and the powerful lure of a semi-pagan environment are coupled with a confused mind and underdeveloped will; teenagers badly need the wisdom and courage of the Holy Spirit.[6] The second drawback comes from the state of mind of the average teenager: at the age of sixteen to eighteen, when most teenagers are in the throes of the manifold turbulence of adolescence, many struggle with belief or suffer from the gnawing pain of a guilty conscience. At this age, they are perhaps even less capable of making a mature decision than younger children.

At the age of thirteen or fourteen, although the inner turmoil is just beginning, the kids do not yet have the car key in their pockets and thus cannot immerse themselves as easily in the allurements of the outside world.[7] In my experience, young teenagers sense at this age the coming storms, and most of them are willing to strengthen themselves in advance with the gifts of the Spirit of God. They have not yet lost their sensitivity to the gentle invitations and consolations of grace.

Administering confirmation to children as soon they reach the age of reason and before they have received their first Holy Communion has the advantage of preserving the traditional order of the sacraments of initiation. Confirmation, again, enables us to receive the Lord more fruitfully in Holy Communion. Even if children at six or seven years old understand much less the significance of confirmation than young teenagers do, we can make them aware later of the powerful resources they have received from God to fight the good fight of adolescence.

[6] It is true that God can and does provide the necessary graces to those who ask for them even outside the actual reception of the sacrament, but this fact does not dispense us from the duty of using the ordinary means of grace that God has made available for such needs.

[7] They have, of course, the virtual world already in their pockets, but parental control (in the case of caring parents) is still easier at this age than it is later.

For these reasons, I recommend that confirmation be administered earlier, either at six to seven years or at thirteen to fourteen.

The Holy Eucharist

In chapter 3, we already discussed the importance of the Eucharist in the prayer life of the priest, so here our focus will turn to the attitude of the priest—both interior and exterior—during the celebration of the Mass. In his book *The Spirit of the Liturgy*, Joseph Cardinal Ratzinger points out that when the priest faces the people during the celebration, his attitude and movements may easily become the center of attention instead of God. Therefore, Ratzinger recommends placing the crucifix upon the altar so that people's attention will be naturally focused not on the priest but on Christ.[8] Still, not even a large crucifix can make the priest invisible, and even if it could, it would also hide the Eucharist. Therefore, we priests need to ask sincerely for the grace that our gestures, voice, and body language may express and inspire worship in the congregation rather than personal attention.

1. How to Speak at Mass

Even the priest's tone of voice affects the mood of his listeners. If it is artificial and contrived, people will complain: "Why does he have to posture? Can't he be more genuine?" Some priests believe that people expect them to be

---

[8] See Joseph Cardinal Ratzinger, *The Spirit of the Liturgy*, commemorative ed. (San Francisco: Ignatius Press, 2018), ch. 3. Alternatively, it is possible to turn back the altar to face the wall of the sanctuary—ideally toward the East, *ad orientem*, from where Christ, the Sun of Justice, rises upon us.

holy, and they attempt to fulfill their expectations by appearing more pious than they truly are. The unctuous style alienates especially those down-to-earth rare church-goers who already suspect that priests do not believe in what they preach. "They are trained to sound pious", many think or say. There is also, however, the opposite danger. In the effort to avoid false piety, other priests try to sound casual and colloquial in order to appear natural. Yet even this can feel inauthentic, and besides, most people do not come to church to listen to a coffee-shop chat. In one way or another, people want to be uplifted. As a reaction against the postconciliar fad of ridiculing clericalism and deemphasizing the leadership of the pastor, we also find old-fashioned young priests who assert their superior status by commanding their parishioners to "stand" or "kneel" in a tone of voice as if they were controlling unruly teenagers.

Public speaking coaches certainly can help in a few pathological cases, but the real problem is not in the vocal cords. If the priest prays and meditates regularly, if he becomes acquainted with the consuming fire of God's Word, and if he strives to love his people with the very love of Jesus, he will find his own natural voice. When he proclaims the Gospel, his personal ambition will be to lose himself in letting the text itself address the congregation. When he recites the prayers of the Mass, he will turn them into his own personal prayer; in other words, he will give voice to the prayer of the Church.[9] As he speaks in the first-person plural of these texts, he includes the community with himself, joining them to Christ and, through

[9] It is not just a legal violation to change the words of the prayers, but a theological mistake, bending the nature of the Eucharistic Prayers: they are the property and the expression of the Church universal, by which the local church manifests her own nature as the local embodiment of the universal Church.

Christ, to the entire Catholic Church. He praises, thanks, and petitions the Father in their name, not just his own.

2. Consecration and Holy Communion

After the prefatory prayers and the invocation of the Holy Spirit, the priest recites the account of the institution of the Eucharist. Here, while pronouncing the words of Consecration, he represents Jesus Himself. Yet it is important to remember that even the institution narrative is prayer (part of the anaphora or the canon), not a magical formula in which the precise pronunciation of each sound is required for validity.

The time between Consecration and Holy Communion is the most sacred time within the Mass, because the crucified and risen Lord Himself is on the altar. Right after recalling the different stages of the mystery of Christ[10]—His Passion, Resurrection, and Ascension (as well as His Second Coming, in the Third and Fourth Eucharistic Prayers)— the priest, along with the congregation, enters into the "once and for all" self-offering of Christ on the Cross to the Father. We join our contrition, praise, and thanksgiving to Christ's perfect praise, thanksgiving, and expiation.

With the recitation or singing of the Our Father, there begins the preparation for Holy Communion in which priest and faithful are to seal their sacramental union with Christ in His self-offering. In every Holy Communion, the entire Christ is offered to us, but we only share in Him to the extent that we are open to this infinite gift.

[10] The Eucharistic commemoration (*anamnesis*) is not simply a subjective act of calling an event to memory. In the words of Saint John Paul II: "In this gift [of the Eucharist] Jesus Christ entrusted to his Church the perennial making present of the paschal mystery. With it he brought about a mysterious 'oneness in time' between that *Triduum* and the passage of the centuries." Encyclical letter *Ecclesia de Eucharistia* (April 17, 2003), no. 5.

The procession to the altar during Holy Communion represents our lifelong pilgrimage, in a communal reenacting of Elijah's journey to Mount Horeb on the strength of the food given him by God. Music at Communion, when it is present, expresses our joy at what we receive.

The *General Instruction of the Roman Missal* recommends a pause between Communion and the post-Communion prayers, leaving time for the faithful to praise and pray to the Lord in their hearts after receiving the Eucharist.[11] Yet in many churches, the priest stands up just as soon as everybody has received Communion to conclude the Mass, leaving no time for quiet prayer. In some places, the lector even begins to read the parish bulletin before post-Communion. We perhaps do not realize that such routines damage the eucharistic piety of our people. We should try to ensure—by singing to Him in community and leaving a silence for personal intimacy—that the reception of Holy Communion will truly unite us both with Jesus and with each other.

3. Adoration

In the nerve-wracking speed of modern life, priests are often forced to "squeeze in" the Mass between other urgent activities, and they are easily tempted to let it become a

---

[11] "Sacred silence also, as part of the celebration, is to be observed at the designated times. Its purpose, however, depends on the time it occurs in each part of the celebration. Thus within the Act of Penitence and again after the invitation to pray, all recollect themselves; but at the conclusion of a reading or the homily, all meditate briefly on what they have heard; then after Communion, they praise and pray to God in their hearts. Even before the celebration itself, it is commendable that silence be observed in the church, in the sacristy, in the vesting room, and in adjacent areas, so that all may dispose themselves to carry out the sacred action in a devout and fitting manner" *The General Instruction of the Roman Missal* (Washington, D.C.: United States Conference of Catholic Bishops, 2011), no. 45.

more or less mindless routine. If nothing else, this difficulty to *pray* our Mass in the moment should awaken in us the need for eucharistic adoration, which deepens our interior link to the Sacrament. Indeed, personal participation in the Mass and adoration outside the Mass are intimately connected, and not only for priests. Our faithful also desire to spend more time before the Lord and speak with Him. Fortunately, adoration of the Blessed Sacrament is spreading everywhere in the United States; in some parishes, a twenty-four-hour chain of worshippers prays every day before the Eucharist. Wherever it takes root, parish life is reinvigorated, and priestly and religious vocations multiply. We priests can do so much to teach our people this wonderful devotion by our example and our commitment to the Lord in the Blessed Sacrament, helping them to appreciate time spent in adoration.

CHAPTER 6

Reconciliation

Christ desired to reach beyond the confines of His earthly life in order to extend His ministry of forgiveness in the Church through all times and places. "If you forgive the sins of any", says Jesus to the apostles, "they are forgiven" (Jn 20:23). To this end, He established not only the Sacrament of Baptism, but the Sacrament of Reconciliation. Whereas baptism can be thought of as the sacrament of the first conversion—it communicates the forgiveness of Christ and the new life He offers to those who enter the Church—reconciliation, or penance, is the sacrament of an ongoing conversion for the forgiveness of the sins we commit after being baptized.

Sin and Guilt

Priests and devout Catholics today often complain about the drastic decline in confessions over the past few generations. The causes of this dwindling are many, but one reason is a diminishing awareness of sin and guilt, both in our people and in our clergy, not to mention in the Western world more generally. Even in Catholic homilies, the word "sin" is rarely mentioned, let alone explained. Seminarians are often told that they must be "positive", that they ought to talk about love, community building, the elimination of poverty, God's mercy, and our resurrection to eternal happiness, rather than the negative drain of sin. Furthermore, they are taught to disprove the widespread myth of "Catholic guilt", replacing the word "sin" with "fault", "imperfection", or "weakness". And where there is no sin, there is no need for confession.

Yet we know that Christ came to call not the righteous, but sinners (Lk 5:32). "If we say we have no sin, we deceive ourselves, and the truth is not in us" (1 Jn 1:8). We need to relearn the reality of sin in the light of the Cross. We need eyes that see what human sins—our very own sins— have done to a God Who handed Himself over into our hands. Then perhaps we will be shaken that God wanted to show, in His own tortured human body and soul, what is the true aim of every sin: the elimination and murder of God. Whenever we commit a grave sin with full awareness and freedom, we overrule God's will. "I know", we say, "that God prohibits what I plan to do because He judges that it is bad for me. But I believe and decide that this act, at least today"—let's say an extramarital escapade— "is good for me." Of course, hardly anybody reflects in such detail on the implications of his sin, but all who consciously sin are aware that they overrule God in that act. To claim to know better than God implies that we ourselves want to be "god" above Him. In other words, we do not want the true God to exist.

Such an understanding of sin and guilt is perhaps difficult for many Christians to bear. It strikes them as overdramatized, or perhaps too graphic. Still, even though people in our age do not like to talk about sin, they are often ready to admit that frequent and deep alienation or *estrangement* is one of the great problems in human life, particularly modern life. This estrangement is, I believe, a symptom of sin, and understanding it can help us to grasp sin more existentially. By sinning, we seek to become what we are not: an absolute being, a god. As a result, in breaking with reality, we distort our relationships with ourselves, with other people, and with God—a threefold rift. This experience is so painful precisely because it goes against human nature. Curiously, sin carries in itself its own punishment. Let us try to look more closely at sin from the perspective of this triple estrangement.

1. Sin as Estrangement from Self

The conscience of a man offers him his highest dignity: when he hears the voice of his conscience, he is called upon to do what is good for the sake of goodness. And that call represents an absolute obligation, an obligation that transcends the man himself. When he listens to this voice and acts on it, he comes most fully alive and becomes, in a sense, most fully himself. Consider an Army medic who sees one of his men fall in a firefight. Is he more himself when he stays put to secure his own life or when, after seeing a way forward, he risks himself to go treat that hurt soldier? It is perfectly accurate to characterize the conscience as one's better self.

Perceiving the call of his own conscience, man at the same time understands that he is free. He alone has the power and the freedom to decide to do the good. Thus we can understand more clearly what happens when a person sins. By contradicting or denying his better self, the judgment of his conscience, the sinner introduces a tragic split into the very center of his own being. He chooses to do what, in reality, his own self has counseled him against. Predictably, once he has sinned, that better self reproves the sinner and, whether he admits it or not, he feels guilty, torn, inwardly divided. Perhaps without even knowing why, the sinner feels as if he is somehow at war with himself.

2. Sin as Estrangement from Our Fellow Man

In acting as if he were the center of the universe, the sinner—consciously or unconsciously—looks at other people as useful means to further his own interests or as dangerous competitors to be eliminated. As a result, he loses his capacity for true personal relationships, to find joy in the joy of his friends. Typically, the older sinners become, the more they find themselves resented and lonely.

Thus, sin carries in itself yet another kind of punishment. The same effort by which the sinner tries to obtain power over others deprives him of their respect and love.

3. Sin as Estrangement from God

By rejecting God's will, sinners exclude themselves from God's friendship, much as someone who double-crosses a human friend sets himself outside that friendship. Yet because every man is created for communion with God, losing the ability to love God means losing happiness. This loss may manifest itself, in the beginning, as an acute sense of emptiness and anxiety, though as time passes, the sinner may come to feel only a vague sense of dissatisfaction and restlessness.

How can friendship with God be restored? The sinner cannot hope to restore the friendship on his own. The nature of human personal relationships should tell us this. When I betray my friend's trust in me, I cannot earn it back, no matter how hard I try. Friendship is a gift, freely given, not a right to which anyone can lay a claim. I cannot prove to anybody that I deserve his friendship. Likewise, if I lose someone's friendship, only that person can give it back to me. If this is the case with human beings, how

much more must it be true about the friendship between
God and man? No matter how much the sinner tries, he
cannot hope to reinstate himself into God's friendship by
his own efforts. Only God can forgive the sinner and bring
him back into His friendship.

A second point to note here is that, as we have seen,
sin has a distorting effect on human *nature*. It makes one
self-absorbed, self-indulgent, and conceited; the person
becomes different from what he was intended to be—a
loving child of God. Only the Creator of that original
nature can heal the distorted person. Only He can restore
us to unselfishness, self-control, and humility.

The Foundations of Confession

Even those who do believe in the reality of sin and the
need for forgiveness can have doubts about the Sacrament
of Penance. We priests often hear the objection: "Why do
I need to go to confession? Why must I go through a middleman, another sinner, to speak to God? After all, only
God can grant me forgiveness. Why can't I go directly
to God to be forgiven?" This is, of course, a valid question. Yes, before everything else, we have to go to God
directly, personally, for forgiveness. Priestly mediation
is totally ineffective unless the penitent first responds to
God's inspiration, examines his conscience before God,
and begs for His mercy and pardon. But within this frame,
the Sacrament of Confession is crucial, and it rests on biblical, historical, and theological foundations.

1. Biblical Foundation

The decisive reason why we need this sacrament is the
simple fact that Jesus Himself gave it to His people. We

will examine a few texts of Scripture that reveal its institution by Jesus and its practice by the apostolic Church.

In the Gospel of John (20:19–23), Jesus presents the entire post-Resurrection mission of the disciples in terms of forgiving and retaining sins. The passage begins, "On the evening of that day, the first day of the week ... Jesus came and stood among them." John relates this as the first appearance of the risen Christ to His disciples.[1] On this first day of the week, this special Sunday, a new creation is established; this day marks the beginning of a new age, the kingdom of the Risen Christ, visible only to the eyes of faith. And on this day, Jesus has a gift for his disciples: "'Peace be with you'", He said. "When he had said this, he showed them his hands and his side. Then the disciples were glad when they saw the Lord. Jesus said to them again, 'Peace be with you'" (Jn 20:19–21).

In order to appreciate what is unfolding here, we need to understand the word "peace", *shalom* in Hebrew, the same customary greeting that Israeli Jews use today. To offer another person *shalom*, then as now, is to wish upon that person the peace that the Messiah will one day bring, a peace that comprises all the blessings of the new age (see, for example, Is 9:1–6; 11:1–9; Mic 5:1–4). At that blessed time, Israel's infidelities will be forgiven, and God will draw so close to His people that "the earth shall be full of the knowledge of the Lord as the waters cover the sea" (Is 11:9). Because Israel will be reconciled to God when this happens, peace will reign also among different peoples: "They shall beat their swords into plowshares, and their spears into pruning hooks" (Mic 4:3); "they shall not hurt or destroy in all my holy mountain" (Is 11:9).

---

[1] In the fourth Gospel, the disciples mentioned after the Eucharistic discourse are the Twelve; here, however, Judas and Thomas are missing (cf. 6:66–71; 20:24).

In the Johannine narrative, Jesus twice speaks the word *shalom* to His disciples. He does not merely wish them peace; He bestows it upon them. During the Last Supper, He had assured them, "Peace I leave with you; my peace I give to you" (Jn 14:27). And this peace summarizes and incorporates *everything* that Jesus gives them. Next, showing them His pierced hands and wounded side, Jesus indicates to them that this peace was the hard-won fruit of His suffering and death on the Cross. Through His death, we now have, firstly, peace with God; secondly, peace with ourselves, since our consciences no longer condemn us; and finally, peace with one another.

The disciples, that tiny band which became the Church, received from Christ this all-important *shalom*. Whoever enters their community enters a community of peace and thus of reconciliation. Although someone already within this community might find himself sinning again—and estranged—these sins can be washed away before God within the loving communion of the Church (see 1 Jn 1:7–10; 5:13–19). Jesus Himself gives the Church this blessing and authority: "'As the Father has sent me, even so I send you.' And when he had said this, he breathed on them, and said to them, 'Receive the Holy Spirit. If you forgive the sins of any, they are forgiven; if you retain the sins of any, they are retained'" (Jn 20:21–23). With these words, Christ commissions His disciples to continue the same work that He received from the Father. In fact, John's Gospel characterizes the entire mission of the Church as transmitting the peace of Christ, the forgiveness of sins, and divine life. This is not something the disciples could have ever hoped to accomplish on their own; it is brought about through the Holy Spirit Who, given by Christ, lives within them.

Jesus does not exclude anyone from the chance to obtain forgiveness, not even those within the Church who sin after baptism. Still, the Johannine text of 20:19–23 does not explain how this reconciliation is to be administered. For guidance on this point, let us look to the Gospel of Matthew: "Truly, I say to you, whatever you bind on earth shall be bound in heaven, and whatever you loose on earth shall be held loosed in heaven" (Mt 18:18). The Church must not only loose, but also bind. What might this mean? Grave sin on the part of a Church member requires some form of excommunication—an exclusion from the communion of peace—so that both the sinner and the community may clearly understand that the sinful member has rejected the life of the Holy Spirit Who unites them.[2] After all, whoever gravely sins has, in effect, become a dead member of the Body of Christ. An instructive example of this process appears in 1 Corinthians 5:1–5, where Saint Paul, in the name of Jesus and by His power, casts out of the community a man who has committed incest. Paul does this in order to promote the sinner's eventual reconciliation; he must be excommunicated "that his spirit may be saved in the day of the Lord Jesus" (see also 2 Thes 3:13–15; 1 Tim 1:19–20). Indeed, if a sinner repents and expresses his sorrow by confessing to a priest, who can bind and loose, the Church will lift the ban of excommunication and readmit him to the community. Notice that this reconciliation with the Church obtains for the penitent God's forgiveness as well. The sin is loosed *in heaven*. Through the Church, Christ prays for the penitent's readmission, which will be more than just an external, earthly act. Absolved of sin, the sinner may again become a living member of the mystical Church, filled with the Holy Spirit (see 1 Jn 5:16).

---

[2] This is not the juridical act of excommunication for some especially grave sins, but the exclusion from Holy Communion for any subjectively mortal sin. Only the Holy Spirit can worthily receive Christ, but the person in the state of mortal sin has banned the Spirit from his soul.

In short, the mediating presence of the Church—and of her priest—presupposes direct contact between Christ and the sinner, and she seeks only to intensify this contact even further. The mediation of God's forgiveness through the priest leads afterward to a renewed direct relationship to God. The prodigal son, the forgiven penitent, can now enjoy the loving embrace of his Father. Thus the priest is not a middleman who stands between God and the penitent but the catalyst of direct personal intimacy between God and man.

2. Historical Foundation

While the shape and practice of this sacrament have undergone some dramatic changes over time, its essential elements remain remarkably consistent with their New Testament origins.

For the first six centuries of the Church, excommunication and reconciliation were strikingly public acts. Indeed, "public penance" is the technical term for the sacrament as it was practiced at that time. Someone who had committed a serious sin would confess it to the bishop, who then excommunicated the sinner by assigning him to the ranks of the penitents. The works of penance given to the penitents might last for many years; in some dioceses, certain sins carried an excommunication and penance that ended only on one's deathbed. The penitential works included fasting and wearing a penitential robe, as well as standing at the Church door or a designated place within the church during Mass to request prayer from the rest of the faithful. In no case was a penitent allowed to receive Holy Communion.

The Church did not by any means abandon these penitents, however, but continued to pray for their conversion. According to Saint Ambrose, "the whole Church takes upon herself the burden of the sinner in order to suffer with him in weeping, prayer, and mourning."[3] When the bishop believed that the penitent had been healed from the spiritual illness of his sins through penance, he readmitted him into full communion with the community. The reconciliation usually occurred on Holy Thursday. With all the penitents present in church, the whole congregation prayed for them as the bishop presided; the bishop then placed his hands on the penitents one by one, and they were allowed to take their places again within the congregation. The Church believed that sinners obtained forgiveness through this penitential process as a whole: namely, the penitent's own acts and the intercession of the community, presided over by the bishop. The process offered simultaneous reconciliation with the Church and, through the Church, with God.

There are a few advantages to this ancient practice. For one, it emphasized that baptism obligates the Christian to live a holy life. Having been washed clean at baptism, and given a new life in Christ, the Christian ought to cherish and develop this life rather than allow it to be destroyed by sin. Losing the presence of the Holy Spirit by serious sin means that the Christian no longer appreciates God's gift. For the Church to believe in the sincerity of this second conversion, the penitent had to prove it to himself and to the Church with long-term acts. Another advantage of public penance was that it had a fundamentally ecclesial character. Far from being a mere legal matter, one's relationship with the Church was a matter of life or death. By losing the Holy Spirit, the sinner became a dead member of a living organism: the Body of Christ. The ancient practice also underscored the connectedness of the members

[3] *De Poenitentia*, bk. 1, no. 81 (translated by author).

of the Church. One could pray and expiate for another. Readmitting the penitent into the congregation required the prayer of the entire local Church, presided over by the bishop. In summary, the early practice of reconciliation emphasized the close link between being reconciled with the Church and being forgiven by God. It recognized that communion with the Church—provided that the sinner is repentant and manifests his sorrow in actions—obtains God's forgiveness.

But there were undesirable aspects of this early form of penance too, which led to its reform. In the Western Church, the prevailing principle was "one baptism, one public penance". The Church believed that if second and third chances were allowed, public penance would lose its seriousness. This caused many people to postpone confessing their sins, for fear that if they relapsed, there would be no second chance. In fact, some bishops counseled young people not to seek public penance, lest they run out of "tries"; instead, they were told simply to confess their sins to God and do penance privately, without involving the bishop. This alternative approach, however, obscured the need for the Sacrament of Penance and created disagreement and confusion among both clergy and lay people. Yet the Gospels themselves spoke clearly: Christ's unlimited mercy required that His disciples forgive an offender "seventy times seven" times. Ought man be less generous than God?

A way out of the dilemma appeared in the sixth century, when Irish monks introduced into Europe a practice of offering reconciliation several times to the same penitent and assigning shorter penances. While this new practice met with strong resistance from regional synods of bishops on the Continent, it gained virtually universal acceptance by the eighth century. Other changes appeared in the Middle Ages. People began to realize the benefits of frequent confession, even for daily venial sins. Furthermore, the faithful now received absolution immediately after confession, even before performing penitential works.

When the modern Church re-examined the Sacrament of Penance after Vatican II, she tried to synthesize the best of ancient and medieval practice. On the one hand, the Church maintained the medieval insight that the sacrament exists for the forgiveness of all sins, including daily venial sins; thus, the sacrament should be used frequently. At the same time, recalling the valuable lessons of the first six centuries, the post–Vatican II Church also insisted that the ecclesial character of the sacrament must appear more clearly. This is achieved today in communal penitential services, when the entire congregation prays for each other during the process of individual confession and absolution.[4] Of course, excommunication for mortal sins—until contrition, confession, and absolution have restored the sinner—has remained constant throughout the entire history of the Church, including today. Mortal sin excludes the sinner from Holy Communion, which is the very heart of the Church.

3. Theological Foundation

The theologian's task is to examine Christ's words and acts and then, as far as possible, explore the reasoning behind them. Having looked at the biblical evidence for Christ's institution of confession and then at its historical development, we are now prepared to ask: *Why* did Christ, Who has done everything in wisdom, establish this sacrament?

---

[4] Only in case of grave pastoral necessity, for instance, before exposure to mortal dangers when no individual confessions are possible, is it allowed to provide—after communal expression of contrition—general absolution with the injunction that the penitents should confess even these forgiven mortal sins at their next individual confession.

Answering this question may be easier if we approach it from three different perspectives: the nature of man, the nature of sin, and the nature of the Church.

1. *The nature of man*. We know that man is neither spirit nor body alone. He is a substantial unity of soul and body. Put more simply, he is an embodied spiritual being. The result is that he expresses inward feelings outwardly, through physical symbols, gestures, and sounds. The same kind of outward signs enable him to receive the spiritual communication of others.

Furthermore, man is a social creature. He depends on other members of the human community for his survival and growth, his physical and spiritual well-being. As an example, a child cannot learn what is right and wrong, or know what it means to be forgiven by other people, unless his parents or others help him to experience these spiritual realities.

The way of our salvation has been purposely designed by God to suit our unique physical and spiritual nature. Thus, in the Sacrament of Penance, our inward sorrow and readiness to change are expressed in words and actions (verbal confession, acts of penance), and we receive the assurance of God's forgiveness through the spoken words of another human being: the priest.

2. *The nature of sin*. Every sin wants to "crawl underground", to stay hidden from us, from God, and from the world. We know that the temptation of every sinner is therefore to rationalize, that is, to hide his guilt even from himself. Each of us feels the impulse to deny, forget, or at least "explain" the evil we have done.

In the sacrament, however, I am forced to face the reality of my sins. I have to dig them up, bring them out into the open, and acknowledge them without false excuses. Confessing them offers a first step toward putting them behind me forever. Saint Ambrose shows the need for confession by addressing to the sinner the words of Jesus to the dead Lazarus, whom He calls out from the tomb: "Seeing the heavy burden of the sinner, the Lord Jesus is weeping. He does not let His Church weep alone. He shares the grief of his beloved and says to the deceased, 'Come out'—that is, you who are lying in the darkness of your conscience, in the filth of your sins, in the prison of sinners, come out and reveal your sin so that you may become justified."[5]

3. *The nature of the Church.* The reason Christ established the Church was to make Himself continually available and active among all peoples. That means that the task of every Christian is to build up the community of God in accordance with his own gifts and to make present the love of Christ when and where he finds himself. At work, among friends, in school, and at home, we are charged with bringing Christ's love into the world; for the world can know that Christ's love is alive and active only if it sees Christians inspired by a love it cannot comprehend, a love that points beyond human power.

One consequence of sin is to weaken the Church. Because of sin, the love of Christ will be less effective; it may not reach certain people. As an example, consider the toxic influence that the selfishness or conceit of one person can have—whether through trauma, bad example, or a breakdown in trust—within a family or a community. The spirit of the entire group is endangered by the wrongdoing of a single member. So it is, more mysteriously, with the Church, even when a sin is hidden. This helps to explain why a Christian who has sinned should seek, not just God's forgiveness, but also reconciliation with the Church his sins have harmed.

---

[5] *De Poenitentia*, bk. 2, nos. 54–57 (translation by author).

As the above historical survey has shown, the community that the Holy Spirit is constantly renewing and filling with the light of His love is the Church. He builds up the Church as the Body of Christ. Every unrepentant Christian is a dead member of the Church, a black spot in the Body, a scandal to those who want to follow Christ. Logically, then, if I am that dead member, I should go to the Church and ask her intercession in regaining for me the life and light of the Holy Spirit.

Qualities of a Good Confessor

We all know about cases in which an insensitive, rude, or indifferent confessor has deterred some people from ever going back to a priest. It would perhaps be easier to list all the mistakes so many of us priests have committed—mostly unaware—than to paint the portrait of an ideal confessor. Although we can, and should, study saintly confessors such as Saint John Vianney and Padre Pio, we cannot always imitate them. What for them was a proper and effective way of handling certain penitents would be for us a grave mistake. For example, Padre Pio would, at times, after a few seconds of listening, close the window in the face of a penitent. He could do this because, through a special grace, he was able to intuit a bad disposition, and he sensed that his rude behavior could help the would-be penitent to reach a sincere contrition. If we ordinary priests tried this, we might simply chase away a soul forever rather than help him confess. Once, a young priest started imitating his mentor, Padre Pio, in his home parish by denying people absolution if they lacked the right attitude. When the old Capuchin saw him again, he immediately berated him, "What, do you think you're Padre Pio? I know when to deny absolution. *You've* got to absolve!"[6] What, then, makes a good confessor? Where do we turn for a model? Outlined below are a few generally applicable traits.

1. He needs *common sense* in discerning the personal character of people, in applying moral norms, and in detecting God's presence. He does not need to be a great theologian or a trained psychologist, just to have a sense of reality regarding God, God's will, and man. When priests lack this, it can bring confusion and damage. Imagine, for example, a priest who prides himself on his courage to declare to every penitent who confesses an objectively grave sin, "You are in the state of mortal sin", but who does not consider the penitent's subjective disposition—how much awareness of the gravity of the sin and how much freedom the penitent has. Such an attitude could cause harm to the penitent. A priest must have an interior feel for God's ways. One cannot be tuned in to God without at least a serious striving for holiness.

2. The confessor needs to be aware that he is *a fellow sinner* along with the penitents. In this, he follows Christ Himself. Jesus wanted to be baptized with John's baptism, which was "for repentance", and die between two criminals even though He was personally sinless. According to Saint Thomas Aquinas, Jesus was the most contrite person ever to live because with His infinite compassion—though He understood perfectly the unfathomable horror of our rejection of the Father—He took upon Himself all the sins of the world. Saint Ambrose, while mourning the sinners in his flock, confesses his own sinfulness:

Grant me first of all that I may know how to grieve with the deepest love with those who sin, for this is the highest

<hr>

[6] Gabriele Amorth, *Padre Pio* (Bologna: Edizioni Dehoniane, 2016), p. 51.

virtue; it is written: "You should not have rejoiced over the people of Judah in the day of their ruin; you should not have boasted in the day of distress" (Obadiah 12); but whenever the sin of someone who has fallen comes to light, may I feel with him; may I not condescendingly reprimand him; may I rather mourn and cry over him so that, while I weep over him, I may cry over myself, saying: "Tamar is more righteous [in the eyes of God] than I" (Gen 38:26).[7]

3. Every confessor must share in the disposition of Christ by *accepting solidarity* with the sinner, and solidarity with the Lord Who is wounded by our sins. The confessor can do this to the extent that, as mentioned in number 2, he is sincerely sorry for his own sins; only in this way does he understand the misery of his fellow humans and the evil of rejecting God's fatherly love. Perhaps we cannot cry as John Vianney did over the grave sins of a penitent, but our compassion for sinners and our sadness over their sins will help us find the right words to speak to them. The personal grief and compassion of the great bishop Saint Cyprian moves us even today, seventeen hundred years later:

> I mourn, brothers, I mourn with you and find no comfort in my own personal integrity and health, for the shepherd is wounded more by the wound of his flock [than by the flock itself]. I join my heart with each one of you. I share the weight of your sorrow and mourning. I grieve with those who are grieving. I weep with those who are weeping. With the fallen, I feel I have fallen myself. My limbs too were struck by the arrows of the raging foe; his savage sword has pierced my body too. No mind can remain

---

[7] *De Poenitentia* bk. 2, no. 73 (translated by author).

free and unscathed from the raging persecution. When my
brothers fell, my heart made me fall too.[8]

With some penitents we can show our solidarity by sharing some of our own struggles in which we have overcome a vice. In this way, we can increase their trust in the
power of God's grace and give them realistic hope for an
eventual victory.

4. With God's help, the confessor should be *truly present*
with penitents. We often do not have enough time for
the individual penitent, yet we should never let ourselves
be distracted or, worse, show impatience or irritation. If,
while conversing with one person, we are watching for, or
just thinking of, the next one, our presence becomes com-
promised. The penitent will feel that he was just a number
and that he was not really listened to.

In fact, one cause of decreased interest in confession
in recent years is the old streamlined attitude of Catholic clergy, who tended to expedite the sacrament. In the
"good old days", when long lines waited outside confes-
sionals every Saturday afternoon, priests often drastically
shortened the time spent with each penitent. In 1963,
for example, one respected (and feared) monsignor reprimanded his young parochial vicar for spending an average
of two minutes with each confessant. "If you spend so
much time with each now", he grumbled, "what will you
do at Christmas time?" No wonder that in many places
confession degenerated into a kind of vending machine
transaction: put in the coins of your sins and listen to the
absolution. Those who were seeking healing, the forgiving words of a loving Father, and the deepening of their
spiritual sensitivity often abandoned the practice out of

---

[8] *De Lapsis* no. 4 (translated by author).

frustration. If we confessors want to educate our people about sin and the joy of receiving God's forgiveness, we must not only provide sufficient time for hearing confessions, but give ourselves fully to them.

Only prayer and love can teach us how to be really present in the confessional. Before we hear confessions, we should ask Jesus for the grace to love and accept everyone as He would. He commanded us to love one another as He loved us, and we know that He is pleased if we beg Him to give us the grace to do what He has commanded. After such a preparation, shorter periods of time with full attention might be sufficient.

During retreats or in other situations, we will sometimes encounter people who are in the process of a radical *metanoia*, a real turning of the direction of their lives, a changing of goals and values. In such cases, we need to be available to listen to their life stories rather than just to their individual sinful acts. But here, we should also be discerning. If the penitent just enjoys telling stories, we can gently lead him back to focusing on what is relevant.

5. The confessor should also pray for *discretion*, so that he may say only what God wants him to say—no more, no less. Questions that feed only our own curiosity, especially regarding sexual sins, may irritate the penitent and elicit temptations for us. Of course, in the case of grave sin, we have to ask about the frequency of sins committed, at least an approximation.

ADVICE FOR INDIVIDUAL CONFESSIONS

The priest must remain available for confession as far as possible. The time periods for confession must respond to the needs of the parishioners, and not to the comfort of the confessors. But even outside of established hours, we should always be ready to hear confessions unless they conflict with undelayable or uninterruptible work. The person who asks us outside of ordinary hours might be in grave spiritual need!

Just as important, though, is the *way* we hear confessions. Our words, our tone of voice, our body language (if the confessants see us)—all this reveals who we are, much as the penitents reveal themselves by exposing their wounds. Penitents can become very sensitive and vulnerable in the encounter, and we may be surprised when, for example, they perceive a slight show of impatience as a rejection. At other times, people unknown to us might thank us profusely for the kind and compassionate reception we gave them in confession, when all we remember is that we tried to be human. Their receptors magnify all that we do.

Different people are often helped by different approaches. In what follows I will make some recommendations about treating various kinds of people in confession.

1. "Prodigal Sons"

The "big fish", those who return to the Church after many years and many grave sins, obviously need special treatment. We ought to respond to them with joy and gratitude. We should tell them that God has never abandoned them and has relentlessly pursued them. All that has happened in their lives, whether happy or tragic, God arranged or at least permitted for the purpose of luring back the lost sheep. At times, it has been necessary for God to shock these individuals out of their comfort zones and block their escape routes in order to draw them back to His fatherly embrace. We can never stress enough God's excessive, almost ridiculous, tender and tough love that has finally triumphed in their lives. We should encourage them to rejoice and assure them that we share their happiness.

What a terrible harm a priest could cause if he insisted on a numerically and specifically precise confession for such returning penitents! Obviously, we try to encourage a good and complete confession, but not beyond the confessant's capacity at that point in his life. So we tell him to confess those sins that he knew in one way or another to be against his conscience at the time he committed them. We may also politely ask him some questions, but always in the context of gratitude and kindness.

2. Saintly Souls

The polar opposite to the "big fish" is the Catholic who is courageously striving for holiness and confesses sins that seem so small that the confessor perhaps wonders if they are indeed even venial sins. It happens at times that we are ashamed and wish we would be as close to God as our penitent is. In these moments, we may be tempted to minimize his guilt or even to assure him that what he confesses are not real sins. If in fact they are not sins, we must say so, but more importantly, we need to be aware of the dynamic character of spiritual life. The soul whose life is motivated by a great love for God and for people sees more clearly than we do his state in the eyes of God. With an increase of light, shadows appear more clearly. Saint John Vianney once asked God to show him the real state of his soul, as God Himself saw it, and after God fulfilled his wish, Saint John never asked for it again. God shows us our sinfulness only to the extent that we can endure it. Thus, if a prudent, nonscrupulous person confesses that his love for his brothers, sisters, parents, or spouse is not real enough, if he says that he resisted God's invitation to help out here or there, that he refused to pray when he had the time and God was drawing him to it, we need to take the penitent seriously and encourage him to start the day with a somewhat modified version of Mother Teresa of Calcutta's prayer: "Lord, help me not to refuse You anything today!" In other words: "I want to do not only what You command but also what You only gently ask me to do: 'Would you do it for Me?'" As a saintly monk said before dying from bone cancer that consumed his spine: "We will never regret what we have done for him."

3. Children

In order to prepare a child for a good confession, we need above all else to prepare the parents. We should include instruction on how to educate children within the larger themes of a couple's marriage preparation. In order to illustrate the problem, I like to tell the parents this true story: one of my confreres was hearing the first confession of children. He woke up from his semi-slumber as one of the children confessed that he had committed adultery ten times. The priest stopped him and asked, "Do you know what adultery is?" "No", came the reply, "but I wanted to be on the safe side." Obviously, the boy had studied an examination of conscience leaflet and tried to memorize it. Ideally, parents should prepare their children for their first confession by trying to awaken and form their children's consciences. Little children do not mind such help. In fact, they will be reassured by it. The parents could go through a typical day and examine how the child responded to God's love, how he acted toward his parents, siblings, classmates, and friends.

Both the parents at home and the priest in the confessional can explain to children the great treasure they carry in their soul: the presence of Jesus Himself. We should tell the child the truth: Jesus loves them very much, and He wants them to be good, obedient, kind, and generous. In truth, Jesus is interested in every detail of their lives. Children can give Jesus joy and can sadden Him. Of course, before we tell them this, we must be convinced ourselves that this is true and not a Santa Claus fable. Jesus Himself taught the insensitive apostles how much He cares about children.

Despite Jesus' special warnings, we find priests today who think that their time is too precious to waste on children. How wrong they are. We will discuss this matter more thoroughly in chapter 9 on counseling children and adolescents.

4. Adolescents

For most, teenage years present unique difficulties. Children easily accept a benevolent "law and order" environment. They feel safe if their parents and teachers set clear limits to their freedom and hold transgressors accountable. By age nine or ten, children have figured out their place and role at home and in school, which helps them feel comfortable. In their early teens, however, the harmony and predictability of their world begins to crumble. They do not understand their unpredictable mood swings, their growing resentment against parental control, or their parents' nervous anger at their questionable behavior. An increase of sexual fantasies and arousals, anxieties, and occasional mad romantic attachments fill them perhaps with shame and guilt while at the same time luring them into the mysterious world of intense pleasure. Girls commonly pass through this period more with secrecy than with dramatic confrontations. Boys, on the other hand, tend to act out and often develop the habit of masturbation and of watching pornography, now incredibly accessible via the internet. We will deal with this particular issue later in this chapter, noting also how habit can compromise the freedom of the will and mitigate the subjective gravity of mortal sin.

In direct contact with adolescents in the confessional and in counseling, we as priests can point out the challenges and the beauty of this period in their lives. This is the time when they discover their freedom of the will, its power and its dangers. We can help them comprehend that their will cannot be manipulated or forced by any external or internal force. Although they may have competing desires and impulses, they possess the power to choose freely which of the many competing forces to accept or resist. We can tell them: "*You*, and nobody else, are the cause of your free act. *You* decide which of the contrasting voices you want to follow." I like to quote to them the powerful lines of Horace: *Si fractus illabatur orbis, impavidum ferient ruinae*; in loose translation: "If a crushed world should fall in upon him, the ruins would strike him undismayed."[9] Thus, nobody and no force, not even the threat of a nuclear strike, can coerce them to commit sin unless they themselves want it. In this way, young men and women can experience the joy of overcoming their fear, their lust, and their gluttony; they see that they can master themselves to the extent that they unite their will with the will of God.[10]

Many teenagers never even discover, let alone build up, the power of their free will. They give up their freedom before they have developed it. Their independence from

---

[9] *Odes*, bk. 3, ode 3, in *The Works of Horace*, trans. C. Smart (London: George Bell & Sons, 1888).

[10] The most difficult struggle in teenage years is the acceptance, the conquest, and finally the integration of sexuality. I deal with this topic in the chapter on marriage.

their parents simply turns into an eager slavery to the latest fad. Unless they wake up later, their behavior will follow either the ways of the majority or those of the impulsive rebels who oppose the majority. In their lives, independent personal choices based on a well-formed conscience will be rare, or not nonexistent.

We should be able to educate our youth so that they may understand how their most noble desires are awakened and nourished by the moral teaching of the Church. Many young people are attracted by the experience of obtaining real inner freedom from the chains of material goods and from slavery to lust and power. They want to serve a cause greater than themselves. We can help them find their "vocation", professions that promote the common good rather than just their own interests.

While a confessor can certainly help teens to develop morally and spiritually, instilling in them a love of God's goodness and mercy, the question of education and parental involvement is as central for adolescents as it is for children. In this time of internal, and at times external, turmoil, the loving and firm presence of the parents is absolutely indispensable if they want to promote a happy outcome for their teens' struggles. These concerns are addressed in chapter 9.

5. Adults in the Professional World

Successful adults, especially in their twenties, thirties, and forties, tend to focus so much on earthly goals, career, income, prestige—the best of them also on their families—that this life seems to them the only reality. Oftentimes, even if they are religious and their faith influences their moral and social life, they think very little about what happens beyond the grave. Still, if they go to church and to the sacraments, a confessor can show them how attractive and fulfilling a truly Christian life can be. If we help them come to believe not just theoretically but existentially that the fullness of life, the real life, begins only after the world no longer sees them—as Saint Ignatius of Antioch said about his own life—their earthly life will become much richer and more meaningful. Saint Thomas More said that he wanted to find joy in every minute of his life, and he proved his sincerity when, putting his head on the block, he quipped to the executioner: "Please do not cut my beard. It did not commit high treason." Yes, we can find joy, or at least peace, in every situation if we try to use it for expanding and deepening our love of God and men. There is no mental or physical pain, joyful or hurtful event, that we cannot turn into a blessing, into an increase of love, if we offer it with Christ to God.

Many people, however, find themselves at one time or another in very challenging situations. People may find themselves in a job that requires them to do what their conscience prohibits: a hospital requires doctors to provide abortion or contraception; a company obligates its employees to participate in unethical business practices; politicians are lured into promoting an immoral cause just because their constituents pressure them. The choice often boils down to disregarding your conscience or losing your job. In such moments, the words of Jesus become a personal call: "Whoever would save his life will lose it; and whoever loses his life for my sake and the gospel's will save it" (Mk 8:35). Every Christian is offered a share in the Cross of Christ.

Even if they do not have to face a drastic choice between God's will and the demands of their jobs, more subtle temptations are waiting for them. For instance, they may have to choose between a promotion that would permit them less time for their family or a lesser income that gives them more family time. Also, those in positions of leadership in a company or in public life have no choice but to influence those under them in either a positive or negative way. Remaining neutral is not an option, and their work has consequences—perhaps even tremendously good ones. Here is an example from real life. The manager of a group of engineers made a difficult decision to lay off some of the employees at the time of the economic recession in 2008. One of the engineers, however, told the boss: "I understand that you cannot pay me now, but I still would like to work for you because I like the spirit of this group so much." Stunned, the manager came to realize that he had been able to develop a family-like community in his company where his co-workers felt personally accepted, appreciated, and cared for. The paradox, of course, is that such a humane, loving atmosphere in the workplace also heightens productivity. Managers, however, who do not care about the workers' personal needs but only about maximum efficiency might lose both their souls and the productivity of their team. We should help penitents to see the spiritual significance of their own work ethic.

6. Scrupulous People

Sooner or later, every confessor meets scrupulous penitents. There is no mistaking the more serious cases, because their confessions are long and complicated with many questions: "Father, was this a sin? Was it a mortal sin?" They also anxiously rehearse old sins because they are not sure whether or not they have confessed them or, if they have, whether or not they correctly explained them. They torture themselves when preparing for confession, but even after confession they worry about what they may have forgotten. If they frequently come back to the same confessor, they try his patience and kindness to no small extent.

I recommend that after you have patiently listened *once* to the list of sins, questions, and doubts, you try to lead scrupulous confessants to the root of their problem. If you yourself had a period of scrupulosity in your life, you may share some of your experience with them and thus gain their trust. Explain to them that this is a frequent trial for those Catholics who take seriously their spiritual life, their sins and virtues. But their problem is that they believe they can stand in immaculate purity before God and so assure their own salvation. Since they naturally find this impossible, they become paralyzed by anxiety. In other words, they try to justify themselves before God rather than ask God to justify them. I ask them never to repeat their past sins and instruct them to think about the tender love of the Father whenever they do their short examination of conscience. The Father is not a bureaucrat straining over every detail of our sins, but an infinitely gentle and passionately rejoicing Father waiting to embrace us.

If scrupulous people learn more about the heart of God, then before all else they will be sorry for their lack of trust in His heart. Saint Thérèse of Lisieux will certainly help them since, in her childhood, she also struggled with scrupulosity. Later, she wrote that even if she had been a greater sinner than Mary Magdalene, she would throw herself into the arms of Jesus and be certain that He would forgive her. Here is crucial advice for the scrupulous: dare to entrust yourselves to God rather than to your own self-made purity. Where are you more secure: in the arms of God or in your own arms? You can have them read the parable of the Pharisee and the tax collector (Lk 18:9–14) and the various encounters of Jesus with the Pharisees.

Lastly, advise them to go to the same confessor so that he can monitor their progress.[11]

7. Users of Pornography

Easy access to the powerful lure of pornography has created an ever-increasing, and largely unreported, epidemic of addiction especially among men, often starting in late childhood or early adolescence. With porn comes also masturbation, and in many cases both become an irresistible, compulsive, daily occurrence. Often, the addiction changes the entire personality. These adolescents—or even adult men—become self-centered and lose their ability to be fully present to others. Their level of zest and joy diminishes. We can see the change in the way they look at the world: cynicism, a waning interest in friends, and an indifference toward the small and great beauties of nature. In some cases, however, the addicts are able to keep up a cheerful, friendly, and energetic exterior, while secretly and often half-consciously clicking into pornographic websites; once they wake up to what they are doing, they are unable to stop. They live double lives, and often only a traumatic result, such as the inability to focus on studies or work or the inability to be intimate and affectionate with their wives, can move them to seek healing.

In counseling them after their confession, we should focus on the dignity of our bodies, which God created to be dwelling places for the Holy Spirit and members of the Body of Christ. We can recommend frequent confessions, an experienced spiritual guide, the morning offering

---

[11] The confessor should also understand that scrupulosity can sometimes be more of a psychological problem than a spiritual one—a manifestation of obsessive-compulsive disorder. He should therefore not hesitate to suggest that the penitent seek appropriate treatment.

of ourselves and our life to Christ, and the search for pure joys, since the expectation of a pure joy or even a healthy excitement makes it easier to resist temptations. The source of joy may be the company of a good friend, physical exercise, an interesting book, or anything else that draws the attention away from the addiction.

Additionally, just as Alcoholics Anonymous is a very effective treatment for alcoholics, so is Sexaholics Anonymous (SA) for sex addicts. The two groups' methods are very similar: First, you acknowledge your addiction and your inability to recover alone. Then, you surrender yourself to a higher power (God, as you understand Him), tell your story to the group, and ask for their help. By frequent meetings and with the help of one other member who accepts responsibility for you, you start on the way of abstinence from both porn and masturbation. This way to recovery is very effective because it follows God's ways to deal with the sinner: confession, request for the community's help, and mutual support.

For young teenagers, participation in an SA group is not feasible. However, one can find online the computer program Covenant Eyes. This software will send to a partner— preferably a responsible person the user can trust—the list of all the websites you have opened that week, with an evaluation of their nature. The Covenant partner thus sees what you are doing online, holds you accountable, and can help and encourage you if you slip. God loves when His children humble themselves before each other and ask for and provide mutual help.

To pornography and masturbation addicts, we should explain that if they are seriously trying to be freed from addiction, not every relapse is a mortal sin for them, because the freedom of their will is at least partially paralyzed. So if they go to confession regularly (weekly or biweekly), they may also receive Holy Communion in between, after making an act of perfect contrition. Jesus will strengthen and heal their staggering will.

8. People with Same-Sex Attraction

These penitents must be heard with particular care, compassion, and discretion. With them, the confessor needs, above all else, two qualities: natural respect for them as God's children and a serene personal conviction about the truth of the Catholic teaching on sexuality (which is outlined at more length in chapter 7 on marriage and sexuality). If the person with same-sex attraction perceives just the smallest sign of revulsion or scorn in the words or body language of the priest, he will never come back. Equally harmful, however, is the counseling of the priest who is personally unconvinced of the truth of Catholic moral doctrine. Such a priest feels constrained to stand by it, perhaps, but deep down feels that he might represent a hopeless, backward position, destined for overhaul. Neither the harsh nor the unconvinced confessor will help the penitent find lasting reconciliation with the Lord.

The Catholic Church, based on the Bible and on Christian tradition, has always taught (1) that consent to homosexual relations in will or in action is gravely sinful, but (2) that same-sex attraction is not, since the person is not responsible for it. Of course, just as in every area of morality, the subjective gravity of a sin in this area is diminished by lack of sufficient knowledge or a lack of freedom. Homosexuals who grow up in today's society with no deep exposure to Christian teaching—or exposed only to an unconvincing version of it—might develop the conviction that their behavior is only a matter of sexual preference, rather than sin. This might excuse them to varying degrees, depending on whether or not their own conscience still makes them feel guilty and spurs them to reconsider the matter. Just as there are compulsive heterosexuals impaired in their freedom to varying degrees, the extent of freedom in homosexual activity also varies from person to person. Attributing full freedom to every homosexual person would be as naive as claiming that they all act under compulsion. In any case, if someone confesses same-sex activities, we need to explain to him in a loving but unambiguous way the Church's teaching. Truth and mercy go hand in hand. More on this theme can be found in chapter 7 on marriage and sexuality.

Teaching Confession to the Faithful

As we know well, the reception of this sacrament involves five steps: examination, contrition, confession, absolution, and penance. First, we examine our conscience in order to discover our sins. Second, we tell God directly that we are sincerely sorry for our sins, ask for His forgiveness, and promise that with His help we will avoid sins in the future. Next, at confession, we outwardly present the sins and our sorrow for them to a priest, who is a representative of Christ and the Church. Then from the priest we receive God's forgiving word—absolution or reconciliation. Finally, we are given the obligation of doing some penance to show the sincerity of our sorrow, though this penance—usually something simple, like reciting a psalm—is purely symbolic, because no matter how severe the penance may be, it receives its value only when united to the sufferings of Jesus, Who alone satisfied for all the sins of the world. Rather than covering all five steps, let us explore the first two in detail.

1. Examination of Conscience

Examining our conscience should be a daily exercise for laypeople and clerics alike, part of our prayer to end the day. If we neglect it, very soon our conscience will grow less and less sensitive to God's inspirations. When that happens, we may find ourselves preparing for a confession without anything meaningful to confess, not because we are in perfect agreement with God's will, but because our conscience no longer senses what separates us from God.

Christians need to be taught this essential, yet often neglected, practice. Most Catholics do not realize that the Ten Commandments are only the beginning of Christian life.[12] Though these give a necessary basis, Christian life is a life with Christ, a life of listening to Him and following His example. As Christians, we share in the divine life of the Lord; we become His brothers and sisters, as well as children of the Father. Christ offers us a share in His own love and joy so that, to the extent that we participate, the carrying of our cross becomes a light burden. Yet perhaps not everyone has the ears to hear this, at least not at first. After all, when the rich young man asked what he must do to inherit eternal life, Jesus answered with the commandments. Only once the man probed further did the Lord invite him to follow (Mk 10:17–22). But to those who have more sensitive consciences, no matter what their state in life, we should present the Beatitudes and Christ's call to take up one's cross and follow Him.

We priests so often recoil from explaining to our people that Christian morality is not reducible to being a decent and upright citizen. Faith, hope, charity, modesty, gentleness, honesty, purity, generosity, gratitude, prayer: these

---

[12] Apart from the first commandment that calls us constantly to grow in our love for God, the fullness of which we can never attain in this life.

are as important as financial and civic responsibility. While we should certainly teach our people to examine their consciences with the help of the Ten Commandments and the moral commands of Christ—regarding lust, anger, and lying, for example—we should also point them to the deeper reality of God's faithful love and our often subtle infidelities to it. Where have I veered from Christ's humble and courageous example? Where have I been deaf to God's call? Where have I resisted the Holy Spirit? Just as importantly, we should always encourage them to examine their consciences *in prayer*. If we try to comb our souls for sins on our own power, we will not get very far. God alone can truly reveal our sins to us.

Here is the paradox: becoming a Christian means accepting the loss of my own life for the sake of Christ, and yet His yoke is easy and His burden is light. Jesus even helps to shoulder the burden of the Ten Commandments. For instance, falling in love with another woman outside of his marriage may intoxicate a man to the point that he feels unable to exist without this woman. She is his love, his happiness, and life without her now seems meaningless. Yet if this man knows that *Christ* has joined him to his wife, he will accept the apparent loss of happiness as a cross and choose to remain faithful to his spouse. After some excruciating pain, his marriage will reach a new depth, intimacy, and peace. With Jesus, the yoke is easy. Saint Augustine beautifully describes this dialectic of pain and joy in Christian life:

> "If anyone wants to follow me, let him deny himself, let him take his cross and follow me." What the Lord commanded seems harsh and difficult, since he said that anyone who wants to follow him should deny himself. And yet it is not harsh and difficult because he commands it who helps us to carry out what he commands.

For it is true what we say to him in the words of the Psalm: "because of the words of your lips I kept to the harsh way of life." But what he himself said is also true: "My yoke is easy and my burden is light" ... Love makes easy what is harsh in the command....

In this holy, good, reconciled, and saved world, or rather in this world to be saved and now already saved in hope, ... the entire Church follows Christ and tells everyone: "Whoever wants to follow me should deny himself." Not only the virgins should hear it, but also the married women, not only the widows but also the brides, not only the monks but also the married men, not only the clergy but also the laity—the universal Church, the entire body, all the members with different tasks and duties, should follow Christ.[13]

2. Contrition

After we have seen our sins clearly, we must bring them to the Lord in sorrow. But what kind of sorrow, or contrition, is sufficient to receive the sacrament? True sorrow is not feeling sorry for myself, nor brooding morbidly over past actions. Neither is it self-rejection or a loss of self-respect. While feeling low, ashamed, or embarrassed after I have sinned is quite normal, such feelings are not sufficient for the sacrament. It is not enough, either, to feel sorry that I have lost the respect of people I admire. To despise sin because it has caused me to lose both self-respect and the admiration of others is a good beginning, but it will not by itself secure God's forgiveness.

Educating our people about true sorrow is one of the most difficult and important parts of our ministry. Saint Benedict recommends in his Rule that a monk confess his sins with tears to God every day, and yet he expects this

[13] *Sermo* 96 (translated by author).

same monk to run with an open heart and inexpressible joy on the way of God's commandments. This paradox is at the heart of monastic life and, in fact, of any authentic Christian life. Sorrow without joy in God's all-embracing love easily degenerates into self-torture, while joy without awareness of the daily need for forgiveness loses its depth and sincerity.

True sorrow begins when I take an objective look at myself, examining my conscience, judging my own actions as God would judge them. I then turn away from my sins and decide, with God's grace, to unite my will with His. To do so, however, requires a supernatural motivation. Looking deeper into the concept of motivation, we distinguish two types:

Imperfect contrition means turning away from my sins and uniting my will to God's chiefly because I fear God and His punishment. This kind of sorrow suffices for a valid confession. It will not, however, obtain forgiveness for the penitent prior to receiving the Sacrament of Reconciliation. As we receive the sacrament, God takes our imperfect contrition and perfects it; He strengthens our initial goodwill and gives us the grace to love Him.

Perfect contrition means that our motive for sorrow is not fear, or fear alone, but love for God. Perfect contrition secures immediate forgiveness for sins, even without the actual reception of the sacrament, though not without at least an implicit desire for going to confession.[14] The grace of perfect contrition, regretting that we offended God's love, anticipates but does not replace the sacrament. In its actual reception, we are reconciled to the Church, our

---

[14] Implicit desire may exist in Protestant Christians and even in non-Christians who have the will to fulfill the conditions God has set for the forgiveness of sins. In other words, they *would* receive the Sacrament of Reconciliation or Baptism if they knew that God willed it.

sorrow is deepened, our love for God increases, and the healing of our sins' lasting effects progresses.

A further consideration in this regard is the lack of absolute certainty that one actually has perfect contrition. Since feeling love for God is not the same as sincerely loving Him, how can we know for sure that our sorrow is perfectly motivated? For this reason also, it is important to seek out the Sacrament of Penance.

As with examining our conscience, contrition should be a daily act, not something hurriedly done in the last minute before going to confession. Making a habit of being sorry for my sins is a very different thing from constant discouragement or depression. To the contrary, telling God again and again that I am sorry for my sins, and that I want to love Him more, is the way to health, peace, and joy. The more sincere my sorrow, the more God's love renews and uplifts me.

The best description of perfect contrition I have found is in a letter of Father Lawrence Sigmond, a simple, holy monk who shepherded the scattered Cistercians in Communist Hungary on behalf of the imprisoned abbot before he himself was captured and tortured. In this letter of spiritual guidance, he refers to conversations with his thief friends in prison:

> How easily God seems to forgive us. In fact, my pickpocket friends last year objected to that. "It is very strange", they said, "that someone murders a human being"—they themselves ... had only cheated and deceived others or stolen a few things—"and then goes to confession and everything will be all right." "But what if he repented of it?" I objected. They replied, "It is easy to say 'I'm sorry'. He is faking it." That is indeed the problem. Sincere and true sorrow is difficult; one needs God's grace to get to that point. Those pickpockets, none of them

were sorry for what they did; they only regretted that they had not been smart enough to avoid getting caught. The only person who knows true sorrow is the one who has already suffered because of his sin. He is not surprised by God's forgiving mercy; his sin hurts him now precisely because he has experienced God's goodness. Sorrow is a great grace; blessed is the suffering of those who are hurting because they have hurt Goodness itself. This sorrow cleanses the soul. The forgiveness is only the kiss that God gives to the purified soul.

Human beings have a hard time forgiving their fellows; they are afraid that if one forgives, the forgiven person will keep hurting them again and again. God also reckons with this possibility, and still he thinks that forgiveness is the best medicine. The more he gives of it to the sick soul, the more effectively it will recover. That is why Jesus says to the Pharisee: "he who is forgiven little, loves little" (Lk 7:47). This is very beautiful! True, repentance marks only the turning point: the soul has changed direction; it is no longer sliding downward, but begins an upward climb. This, however, is only the beginning! The healing has started, but it takes time until it is complete. The soul still has to follow a diet, take its medication regularly, and breathe much fresh clean air. How long will the recovery take? It depends on many factors, especially on the degree and depth of the sorrow. The complete turning away [from sin] brings about a quick recovery; a half-hearted resolution may easily be reversed. But recovery does not depend only on sorrow. Someone may be fully determined [to turn away from sin] and yet still need time and maturation before the more deep-seated centers of pus burst open. One has to love the light; it is the Sun that heals.[15]

[15] Lawrence Sigmond, letter to a woman from Pannonhalma, Hungary, dated September 7, 1963.

CHAPTER 7

Marriage and Sexuality

Though a priest is not involved in the day-to-day of couples' lives, he can nevertheless play a crucial role. He prepares them for marriage, confers the sacrament, counsels them, hears their confessions, and helps them to educate their children spiritually. He also accompanies people tossed by the waves of human sexuality: divorced people, uncommitted couples, victims of abuse, pornography addicts. In a modern world so charged with *eros*—with such a wild swarm of conflicting ideas about sex and love—this task of the Catholic priest is especially demanding, and tough to navigate. In this chapter, we will address an array of themes touching the complex but ultimately beautiful reality of sexuality and marriage: the theological and existential foundations of matrimony; advice on counseling, ranging from teenagers to couples in a midlife crisis; pastoral approaches to contraception, divorce, and remarriage; and the question of same-sex attraction.

THE PROFUNDITY OF SEXUAL RELATIONS

Premarital and extramarital sex are now commonplace, especially among young adults, even many practicing Catholics. Yet people who have not lost their sensitivity by extreme promiscuity sense instinctively that sexual relations, even outside of marriage, are quite serious, inviting both parties to more than a passing release of lust. In the genital union of a woman and a man, the two feel that they have come to "know" each other in an intimate way, that a tie has been created between them. Whether the couple acknowledges it or not, sex and marriage, the mutual sacramental gift of self before God, are profoundly linked; the vulnerability of the sex act needs the assurance and stability of marriage. How can we help people to recognize this existential reality of sex and see its inherent connection to the Sacrament of Matrimony?

If an unmarried couple is in love, they sense, at least obscurely, that in sex they give "part" of themselves bodily to the other. In most cases, we priests can help them to become aware that their mutual physical giving calls for a personal gift of the self. In fact, if man is a unity of soul and body, how could it be otherwise? Once we accept the truth of this insight, it becomes clear why sexual intercourse outside of marriage is a false act. The "language" of the act says, "I am yours, since my body is yours", but the unmarried lovers' act cannot sincerely mean this, since the two are not committed to each other. At any time they are free to withdraw their gift of self. Moreover, if their union results in conceiving a child, the road will be staggeringly difficult for the couple if they do not wed. Of course, their natural instincts tell them to stay together to nurture and protect the unborn child at least until the time that he is able to have an independent adult existence. But if they do not marry, this instinct does not secure a stable two-parent family, which is necessary for a child's happy and healthy upbringing.

But one might still wonder, "Why isn't a civil ceremony sufficient? Isn't that marital commitment too?" A civil marriage is indeed a commitment—a purely human one. When first falling in love, a couple feels that their romantic, merely human affection will help them always to love one another. But once beauty and desire fade, and there emerge arguments, nagging, illness, financial problems, and the possibility of extramarital liaisons, will the two still be able to stick by their vows and be grateful for each other? How deep will their love go? As the philosopher Gabriel Marcel said: "To love is to say to someone, 'You will never die.'"[1] Can a couple ever obtain such a life for one another, or for their children? Human effort and emotion cannot assure a lifelong, loving marriage open to children, and they surely cannot secure eternal happiness.

If a couple realizes all this, then they know they must look for a power and a love beyond human capabilities. At this point, longing for the *Sacrament* of Marriage begins to make full sense. In this sacrament, Christ offers the couple a share in His perfect spiritual marriage with the Church that He sealed on the Cross.[2] If the couple receives the sacrament, the indissoluble and unconditionally faithful love of Christ for His Church strengthens their efforts for a lifelong, life-giving marriage. He will be present in the couple's daily life (unless they force Him out by mortal sin), and they can always ask for His help. There will be no crisis they cannot overcome with His help so long as both partners ask for it. In the active presence of Christ, a couple can overcome periods of no longer feeling love for one another and realize that, in fact, it is exactly in such times that true love and its sustaining faith can become deeper and stronger. Loving

---

[1] Gabriel Marcel, *L'Emissaire*, in *Vers un autre royaume: Deux Drames des années noirs*, as quoted by Seymour Cain, *Gabriel Marcel* (South Bend, Ind.: Regnery/Gateway, 1963), p. 86.

[2] The spiritual marriage between Christ and the Church (Eph 5:25–27) is *the* perfect marriage; sacramental marriage on earth is only participation in it.

and forgiving each other time and again, they will become channels for each other of Christ's almighty love that prepares them for eternal life.

Out of reverence for God, they will not interfere with the life-giving potential of the marital act. They will preserve its openness toward God the Creator and allow "God to be God", creating new human beings out of love. The parents will also want to raise their children out of love, rather than merely tolerating them as an unwanted liability and burden. In this same love, they will ensure the children's baptism and nourish their faith—a cooperation with God, helping their children share in the eternal life and joy of Christ.

Biblical Teaching on Marriage

Now that we have seen how much God's help is needed to live up to the dignity and goals of sexual relations, I will briefly summarize the Old and New Testament teaching on sexual relations and God's role in it.

In the more developed religions of agricultural societies, the gods became symbols of inexhaustible biological vitality, and the myths of these societies projected into the lives of the gods the usual patterns of human sexual behavior: fornication, infidelity, and even incest. We could think, for example, of the Canaanite deities, the Hindu Indra, the Hellenic Dionysius, the Roman Bacchus.

In Israel, a quite different process took place. It became clear that Yahweh transcends sexuality and, unlike the pagan gods, needs no sex partner. Sexuality, they recognized, is not a divine attribute but rather belongs to the blessings of God's creation. Once this clarification had been achieved, however, the prophets (Hos 2:1–20; Ezek

16:1–63; Is 54:4–8) and the Song of Songs often applied the metaphor of a loving, forgiving, unconditionally faithful bridegroom in order to describe Yahweh's love for Israel. According to their faith, the Messianic times will be characterized by God's forgiveness of Israel's infidelities and her definitive espousal to God in eternal fidelity and love. The deepened understanding of Yahweh's faithful, forgiving, unconditional love influenced the sexual attitudes of Israel. Monogamy and fidelity are presented as the ideal in Malachi 2:10–17, as well as in Genesis 1–2, and the sixth commandment makes clear the evil of adultery. Since Yahweh remains true to Israel, Israelite husbands should also be faithful to their wives rather than divorce them or betray them.

Christian revelation unfolds the hitherto hidden Christological dynamism of marriage and makes it a sacrament, through which partners share in the love of the Son of God for the Church. The New Testament revelation on sexuality can be understood only against this background. In Jesus, Yahweh Himself came to cleanse and re-create Israel, His unfaithful bride, and inaugurate the Messianic wedding feast (cf. Mk 2:19–20; Jn 3:29; Eph 5:25–32; Rev 21:1–2; 22:17). Christian marriage not only points to this marriage but actually communicates to the couple a share in the Son's virginal, marital love for the Church. Their mutual human love and their sexual relationship are healed and transformed by the same love that creates and nourishes the Church and binds her to Christ. If the couple accepts Christ's love with faith, if they struggle to open themselves to it more and more, it will gradually purify and transform their relationship. In other words, their love for each other will become unconditional, life giving, and forgiving in various ways. This share of spouses in the unbreakable bond that unites Christ and the Church explains why the Church cannot dissolve a sacramental, consummated marriage.[3]

EARLY PREPARATION FOR MARRIAGE

Having described the basic theological foundations of Christian marriage, we will turn now to the long road of personal preparation for marriage, beginning in the murkiest stages of teenage development and ending with the practice of "steady" dating. At every step, even before people have begun dating, the priest can help guide the faithful to a right attitude.

1. Adolescence: Growing in Freedom

The spiritual and psychological maturity necessary for marriage is nourished deeply—though by no means exclusively—by the experiences and trials of adolescence, when, for most people, marriage is not on the immediate horizon. During this time, the young person has an opportunity to gain a healthy autonomy.

The baby in the womb lives in symbiosis with the mother, receiving food and oxygen from her. Since we are psychosomatic creatures, a unity of soul and body, the biological bond of the umbilical cord continues as a psychological bond between mother and child that lasts for years after birth. The child depends on the mother for all his physical needs, as well as trying to imitate and please

---

[3] According to canon law, the Church can dissolve a sacramental, sexually unconsummated marriage for grave reasons. Why sexual consummation makes the marriage absolutely indissoluble, theologians can only speculate: it is both the intention of the mutual offering of the self expressed in the vows and the actualization of this offering in sexual relations that seals the bond definitively between husband and wife.

her, while the mother tends to consider her child as the extension of her own body.

Adolescence is the time when the close bond of dependence upon the mother should gradually give way to mutual love, respect, and a growing autonomy. Teenagers should be given space and privacy and should gradually learn self-reliance, while still obeying and respecting their parents.

In my experience, I have noted that trouble arises if, for some reason, the bond is not allowed to dissolve. Consciously or (more often) unconsciously, an overly possessive mother—especially if she is frustrated in her relationship with her husband—may not be ready to cut the psychological umbilical cord; so she may want to keep her adolescent psychologically dependent on herself. The result is an arrested development of the child's personality: the bond is transformed into *bondage*. Some signs of bondage between mother and teenager include constant fighting (though occasional conflicts are normal), a love-hate relationship, and constant anxiety about each other. If there is indeed a *love*-hate relationship, this will also result in heightened guilty feelings after fights.

What does this have to do with marriage? If a young man still in bondage to his mother begins to date, he will most likely pick a girl who will be a substitute mother for him, older, domineering, yet mesmerizing. The dating relationship will turn into a replica of the love-hate relationship he had or still has with his mother. If he then marries such a substitute mother, he will project upon his wife the qualities he admired and hated in his mother. The result will be an unhappy marriage with unceasing, mutually demeaning fights: they will be unable to live with each other but also unable to live without each other. In such cases, the husband often runs back home to complain to his mother about his wife rather than resolving the conflict together with his spouse.

Clearly, this is not an ideal situation. How can we help as priests? First, practically speaking, we can advise the young man simply to be attentive to this dynamic when dating. If he notices that the bondage is being transferred to his girlfriend, just acknowledging its reality will already help weaken its grip on him, so that he no longer subconsciously transfers the qualities of his mother to his girlfriend, at least not so easily. But if the bondage, the love-hate relationship, and the constant fights persist, the best medicine is to terminate the relationship.

This, however, will not solve the problem. The best way for a teenager to assert his growing maturity is to show respect for his parents rather than provoke a resentful argument. Whereas fights only show that the adolescent has not freed himself from dependence, courtesy and respect for one's parents are sure signs of growing maturity and independence. Courtesy from the child invites respect on the part of the parents. When a teenager treats his mother with respect, he paradoxically creates a distance between her and himself. Certainly, as long as he lives under her roof, he should obey her in matters in which she has the right to his obedience, such as living as part of the family, helping out with chores, and respecting curfews. But neither parent has the right, for example, to prescribe for you what profession you should pursue or whom you should marry. Their advice should be welcomed, but their pressure gently ignored.

2. Adolescence: Discovering Unselfish Love

The greatest challenge for adolescents is to develop the capacity for real, unselfish love. The natural tendency of adolescents is to look into a mirror constantly, watch themselves, and be tossed back and forth between anxiety and self-admiration. They worry about the impression they make on others and about their success or failure in school, athletics, and social life. They long for recognition, honor, influence, and prestige. In order to discover that instead, the only lasting satisfaction comes from loving and being loved, they need time, but above all they need God's grace, which He offers to everyone. When we cooperate with this grace (and this cooperation is itself a grace), it does not necessarily make our struggle easier, but it enables us to win, if we fight sincerely.

Indeed, it takes us a whole lifetime to learn what it means to love *truly*, but the flower can blossom in adolescence. We can teach the rudiments to teenagers. True love values and fosters the beloved's life and growth, while selfish love does the opposite. Selfish love uses the other person for one's own advantage or lust, damaging the personal life and growth of both involved. Briefly put, pure love means sharing and imitating God's love for us. He wants us to exist, flourish, and become happy by sharing in the pattern and the strength of His own love. Gradually, we can learn that loving another person means pledging ourselves to cherish and nourish this person's life according to the reality of our relationship.

3. Casual Dating

Young people often ask priests about dating issues. Here are some common-sense ideas addressed to teenagers and young adults to ensure enjoyable and wholesome dating, of which they need not be ashamed later in front of their spouse and children.

First of all, dating is different for teenagers than for young adults. Some parents are so anxious about their children's heterosexual development that they promote their early dating experiences even at the age of thirteen or fourteen. Responsible psychologists insist that children and young teens need first to socialize and establish healthy friendships among their own sex before they venture out to dating members of the opposite sex. Otherwise, young teenagers will burden their equally young and inexperienced dates with all their confused emotional needs. If such early relationships break up, as they usually do, the lonely teens will have an emotional burden scarcely bearable without the support of mature friends of their own sex. Older teens, however, with a network of healthy friendships and relationships to rely upon, will be better protected against such upheavals.

Even once teenagers begin dating, the goal of dating in high school, or even early in college, is not to choose one's spouse. It is the time for establishing healthy personal relationships with members of the opposite sex and perhaps developing some lasting friendships. Even those who are more prepared to look for a spouse should treat dating with discretion, going against the world's tendency to treat a relationship immediately as a marriage in miniature. Dating—at least before the two are thinking seriously about marrying—is more like friendship than like marriage.

A dating relationship is good if you find it inspiring, if it brings out the best in both of you, if you are both more alive, more yourselves, more noble, more tender in each other's presence. Your friend should draw your attention away from yourself and toward him or her. If, on the other hand, you cannot live a single day without seeing or talking to him or her on the phone, then an unhealthy dependency has developed. You should learn to stand on your own feet and be alone with yourself. Share your emotional problems with some trusted friend or counselor rather than dumping them on your girl- or boyfriend. Unilaterally burdening the other with your problems is not the same as talking about your joys and sorrows to the extent that he or she is really interested. The first is an abuse of friendship; the second is its blessing.

Playfulness and creativity are important. Try alternating the role of leading and being led rather than thinking that the boy always has to take the initiative. Be creative in finding things to do, whether choosing a good movie, play, or concert, or just walking or hiking. If you just drive around and park the car, things can easily get out of hand.

Communication is essential. Instead of trying to impress each other with how clever or educated you are, share some of your interests and experiences. If you have enjoyed such a simple thing as a sunset, a short story, or a good movie, talk to your friend about it. Be yourself rather than play a role or put on a mask. When you reveal your real feelings, including your fears, you become vulnerable to indifference or scorn, but you must have the courage to risk that. Your real self is always more attractive than a mask.

Do not be afraid of being tender, kind, and warm. Only strong people can afford to show their "weak side". Instead of progressing toward more physical intimacy, accept the much greater challenge of becoming a good friend to your date. This will not only be a much more satisfying experience in the present, but will make it possible to remain friends if the dating ends. Show a growing interest in the other, reveal gradually who you are, grow in an exchange of feelings and dreams, goals, and ideas.

Regarding physical contact, remember that the same gesture, whether an embrace, hug, or kiss, can express love and affection for one person and lust for another.

Much depends on the heart, on the intention of the persons involved. In any event, the following rule always applies: avoid not only sexual intercourse but whatever actions are designed to arouse the other sexually. Those physical actions meant to stir up sexual passion are an intercourse in desire (cf. Mt 5:28) and therefore, outside of marriage, seriously opposed to the will of Christ. You have no right to each other's bodies since you have not committed yourselves to each other.

Choose the company of those whose expectations and values agree with yours. If the situation is in danger of getting out of hand, talk it over with your friend and together decide to keep each other chaste. I would tell the man: In every male there are two strong desires—to possess the girl and to defend her chastity. So be her knight and defend her chastity against your own instinct to possess her. Learn to love her beauty as you love an attractive flower. You should not tear it off. Avoid situations in which temptations may become overwhelming. When in doubt, think about the future: What experiences would you be proud to share with your spouse fifteen years from now? Which would cause embarrassment for you and pain to her or him? If you seek emotional sharing and satisfaction, rather than sexual gratification, you will cherish the memory of some of your dates for the rest of your life.

What is true about the possession of material goods is true, analogously, about the "possession" of a person: only if you are ready to renounce all material goods for the sake of Christ does the world reveal its beauty to you, and only then does the world belong to you. In a similar way, only if you renounce the body of your friend every time you have a date can you sincerely admire and enjoy each other—only then can you be at the same time natural, tender, affectionate, and chaste.

Christ came first of all not to promulgate prohibitions but to clean our hearts and transform them. Everything is pure for the one who has a pure heart (cf. Mt 5:8). He who wants to follow Christ will strive for purity not only in his actions but also in his heart. Sexual fantasies and desires often arise spontaneously, especially in men. They are only sinful if, outside of marriage, we seek, entertain, or consent to them. The best way to fight them is to seek pure joys. Only pure joys can weaken the attraction of lust. Good friendships bring the best out of you. Also helpful are intellectual pursuits and hobbies. Physical exhaustion from work or athletics can help to channel or sublimate sexual energies to nobler goals.[4] Purity of heart does not mean being ashamed of one's sexual nature but rather gathering together one's fragmented, uncontrolled drives and instincts and putting them toward a good. The man or woman of a pure heart is like a powerful lens that focuses the divergent rays of the sun; through God's grace, a pure person is able to direct all his energies toward his life's mission. Only someone of pure heart, who is truly whole, can give him- or herself wholly to God and wholly to his or her spouse.

4. Casual Dating Advice for Women

Women, of course, have to be attentive in a special way. If until now I have seemed to discuss dating mainly from the viewpoint of boys, this is because in my priestly life I have primarily counseled high school boys rather than girls. Only in the last five years, after retiring from Cistercian

---

[4] "Sublimating" sexual energies is an amazing process that manifests the unity of the spiritual and biological aspect of the human being. The biological energies of the sexual drive can be elevated and transformed into intellectual-spiritual energies. For instance, continence freely chosen or accepted can increase your intellectual appetite and your loving service to your fellow men and women and inflame the passion of your prayer.

Preparatory School near Dallas, have I begun to give direction to girls at a university. Some priests reading this volume may already have a great deal more experience in this camp, but nonetheless here are some basic recommendations addressed to young women.

Girls, do not trust easily a boy's vows of passionate love, especially when he insists: "If you really love me, please show it to me: let's spend the night together. You don't need to be afraid of me!" As a wise lady told my students, "Boys lie about love in order to get sex, and girls long for love, so they yield to sex." Indeed, girls without previous sexual experience would prefer tender loving care to the "act". Those who have already had multiple partners more easily give their bodies in order to bargain for at least a semblance of love.

Girls who are looking for good young men, capable of lifelong love, fidelity, and true fatherhood, prove their high self-esteem. They know that their bodies and souls are so dear and precious to Christ that He wants to dwell in them as in His sanctuary. If God so highly reveres their bodies, they themselves should imitate this reverence. Such a woman will give her body only along with her soul to a husband who, in turn, gives his body and soul to her in a mutual lifelong commitment.

In every woman there lurks, so to speak, both an Eve and a Mary. She can on the one hand develop into a "temptress", someone who appeals to the lower instincts of the man, his "bad spirit". She may come to enjoy male attention and admiration so much that, for "fun", she dresses provocatively, flirts with boys at parties, or even yields up her body in some way. But then, on the other hand, there are those women who can awaken in their boyfriends their best selves. The boys are themselves amazed by the change, finding themselves gentle and affectionate, eager to surround their girlfriends with little signs of care and service. They want to live up to their girlfriends' expectations. Chastity is much easier in such cases.

In this life on earth, the evangelical ideal of chastity of heart remains a goal toward which we must always strive, rather than a comfortably acquired state on which we can pride ourselves. It is important to pray, struggle, ask for pardon, and never give up. Saint Bernard insists that it is possible for the repentant nonvirgin and adulterer to enter the kingdom, but impossible for the proud Pharisee who does not even realize that he needs forgiveness.

5. Steady Dating

By steady dating, we mean an exclusive and lasting dating relationship (often for several years) in which both "partners" pledge to date only each other. Such a relationship is natural and very helpful as a preliminary to engagement and marriage. But in high school, when marriage is still many years away, steady dating is an unhealthy practice. It narrows down one's chances of getting to know several people and of developing friendships with them. A teenage boy and girl who date each other exclusively for several years will almost necessarily end up in an emotionally tense and confused relationship. They know that they are not married, yet they feel tied to each other so closely that they do not associate with anyone else. Their emotional freedom and growth are stifled. When, almost inevitably, they break up later, both of them will have suffered lasting emotional damage.

If early steady dating is harmful for personal growth, *cohabitation*—widespread in many societies, especially among young adults—becomes an even more serious obstacle to achieving emotional maturity. The usual motive of a couple living together before marriage, or avoiding marriage altogether, is to avoid committing themselves to each other. "How can I know if I will still love my partner after ten years? We want to avoid hurting each other with a divorce. We freely chose not to commit so there will be no cause for guilt or blame if we break up." Often, they have seen the pain of divorced couples, perhaps even in their own families, and they do not want to risk such devastation. But cohabitation does not offer comfort. In reality, the uncertainty of the future, the fear that something as small as an unnoticed irritation, a petty disagreement, or poor performance in bed might lead to a break-up at any time may lead to an increasing lack of trust and a growing anxiety level. Even those who choose cohabitation before marriage in order to ascertain that they are compatible enough will be frustrated. During the trial period, both of them will be on their best behavior, since they know that the relationship depends on performance. But after the knot is tied, they relax and their real character surfaces. Thus, they cannot know each other before they become husband and wife. Statistics show that people who have cohabitated before marriage are more likely to divorce than those who have not.

Counseling Engaged Couples

A priest should accompany the couple through their engagement. The content and tone of these meetings may vary widely depending on the couple—their faith, their education, their maturity, their stability. In any case, they should learn about the spiritual and ethical richness of the Sacrament of Matrimony, which is explored throughout this chapter. They should also be warned of certain pitfalls, both psychological and moral, that may emerge along the way. We will unpack some particularly pressing issues like interfaith marriage, contraception, and divorce later in the chapter. The emphases should correspond to the couple's needs, and ultimately, the priest must use his own discernment and discretion to decide how best to help each particular engaged couple prepare for marriage, without passing over the doctrinal and canonical norms.

1. Immediate Preparation

When a couple gets engaged, they should contact the pastor of the church where they want to be married at least six months before the wedding date. Most churches are booked well in advance. Normally, a Catholic couple gets married in the church of the bride and a mixed couple in the church of the Catholic partner, although exceptions for good reasons can be made.

With such practical questions settled, the best preparation for marriage, besides talking with a priest, is an Engaged Encounter weekend program and a series of visits with a sponsor family. During the Engaged Encounter, the couple is prompted to communicate with each other about matters they had not dared to face before. The sponsor couple, on the other hand, will tell them about their own marriage, their experiences, challenges, joys, crises, and struggles, and how they have benefitted from all of them. It is also useful for the couple to fill out the FOCCUS Pre-Marriage Inventory together, which will help them discuss their agreements and disagreements about various aspects of married life.

2. Agreeing on a Plan for Marriage

Engaged couples need to go into marriage with a common plan. Although Encounter weekends and other marriage preparation programs can help them tremendously, the priest should make sure that the couple is indeed approaching the sacrament with their eyes wide open. A great deal can be done at this early stage to help couples steel themselves against temptations and crises down the road, including an eventual midlife crisis (which we will discuss in the section on counseling for married couples). Here, we will cover a few fundamental points.

Before marriage, it is important for a couple not only to have sexual attraction to each other but also to have developed a deep friendship. They should share some common interests and have a comparable level of education. More importantly, both should have a deep faith in and love for God. They should believe that their marriage is sacred, shares in Christ's unconditional love, and is therefore indissoluble by divorce.

It is essential that engaged couples agree on goals before they marry. The overarching goal, as Christians, should be to grow together in love—love of God and love of each other. They should strive to accomplish this at all times and under all circumstances. To do this together, they need only God, Who binds Himself in the sacrament to give His grace for this exact purpose. And indeed, this purpose is not abstract or unrealistic, but takes the form of small, practical goals lived out in everyday life. The following is a brief list of the kind of simple, concrete things couples should agree on before marriage.

- Agree to pray every day as a couple, as a family. This will strengthen their bond.
- Agree to spend quality time together, possibly every day but at least every week. Remember the story of the husband whom a reporter asked at his golden anniversary, "What is the secret of your long and happy marriage?" "It's very simple", the husband replied. "I took her out every week, candlelight and all that."

- Agree to work together on volunteer projects, either for the parish or for a community organization.
- Agree on whether or not the wife will work after she has children.
- Agree on the size of the family.
- Agree on distributing responsibilities.
- Agree on how to divide household chores if both of them work. It is important that the husband shares in the chores.
- Agree on how to handle finances.
- Agree on how to handle in-laws. As a rule, dependence on one set of in-laws breeds resentment. Keep an equal distance from both sets.

If couples reach harmony on these matters while still engaged, they will have a much greater likelihood of staying faithful and happy together years down the line.

3. Signs of a Bad Engagement

When engaged couples meet with a priest, they should also learn some of the red flags that signal a wrong-footed marriage. We offer here a few important examples:

- If the couple has known each other for less than a year, the chances for divorce are very high.
- If pregnancy has already occurred, this may or may not be an obstacle. If the couple had wanted to get married anyway, there is no reason for delay. But if the pregnancy alone prompted the couple to get married, chances are that the marriage will not survive. In this case, they might consider giving up the child for adoption and not marrying until the child is safely adopted—if they decide to marry at all.
- If one partner is totally dependent on the other, this is a serious warning sign. The partner may have no

will or personality of his or her own, attaching to the other as a "leech". He or she might say, "If you broke off the engagement, I would commit suicide." Such a person can become an unbearable burden through his or her passive-aggressive clinging. Couples like this should be encouraged kindly but firmly to break up.

- Domination is another serious warning sign. One partner may control the other so much as to reduce her or him to a kind of slavery. If the domineering partner is unwilling or unable to change, the chance for a successful marriage is slim.

- If one of the partners is an alcoholic or drug addict, the marriage is heading toward disaster. Getting drunk at least once every ten days is a sign of alcoholism. However, if he or she is able to change before the wedding, there is hope that the spouse will remain sober for the other's sake. As a marriage counselor once said, "If he doesn't change to get you, he won't change to keep you."

- If the woman is older and desperately wants to get married because all of her friends have, the man should discern carefully how much she loves him personally. Men more easily marry in middle age or even later and thus do not succumb so much to the pressure of the clock, but older women may get married without love just for the sake of having children or curing their loneliness.

- If one of the partners is irresponsible with money or unable to hold a job, it does not bode well for the marriage.

Additionally, if a couple does not share the same faith, this can present major problems in their marriage, and they should have full awareness of the challenges and the canonical requirements. This complex issue merits a longer discussion.

MARRIAGE BETWEEN CATHOLICS AND NON-CATHOLICS

The Church has serious misgivings about marriages between Catholics and *non-Christians*. From the start, the couple will be divided on the most important values of their marriage, and their separation in matters of faith will also make the education of children more difficult. Nevertheless, the Church grants dispensation, if requested, under the following conditions: (1) the Catholic party promises to practice the Catholic faith; (2) he or she does all in his or her power to assure the Catholic education of all the children; (3) the non-Christian spouse accepts the obligations of the Catholic spouse; and (4) both marriage partners take part in a preparation sponsored by the Catholic Church. Still, even if a marriage between a Catholic and a non-Christian under such conditions is considered valid, it is not sacramental; only two baptized Christians who have faith in Christ can consciously communicate the love of Christ to each other in the marriage. Weddings between Catholics and non-Christians normally take place in a Catholic church, but in exceptional cases they may also be celebrated outside of a church by the minister of the non-Christian religion or a justice of the peace.

A marriage between a Catholic and a non-Catholic *Christian* is less problematic. Such a marriage is considered sacramental if the Catholic partner obtains dispensation from the Church, under the same conditions as above. The usual way to celebrate the wedding is in the Catholic church of the Catholic partner before a Catholic priest or deacon who has the authority to officiate.

A Protestant minister may be present as well to perform part of the ceremony (preach, pray), though not the reception of the vows. For some serious reason (for example, peace among the families of bride and groom, special relationship of the non-Catholic partner to a church or minister, etc.) the couple may ask dispensation from the "canonical form" so that the marriage may take place in a Protestant church before a Protestant minister. In this case, a Catholic priest may be present and lead part of the ceremony, but not the reception of the vows.

The requirement that the Catholic party do all in his or her power to ensure the Catholic education of all the children may cause some tensions. This condition may appear to the other spouse as an imperialist ploy to acquire new members for the Catholic Church. In reality, this requirement stems from the very nature of the Catholic faith. Catholics believe that only the Catholic Church has preserved the fullness of revelation (teaching, sacraments, and moral principles) that Christ wanted to give to His Church. Naturally, then, Catholics want to transmit to their children this faith, which they believe to be the greatest treasure anyone can have. For the Catholic partner, this is a matter of conscience. In a marriage with a Protestant, this may present fewer problems, since, barring anti-Catholic bigotry, most educated Protestants recognize that Catholics can be good Christians. If the Protestant spouse sees that the religion of the children is a matter of conscience for the Catholic party, he or she will more easily yield since, normally, denomination is not a matter of conscience for non-Catholics. The Catholic partner should, in turn, reassure the non-Catholic that if their children are raised Catholic, they will learn to respect and practice all that the Protestant parent respects and practices—Bible reading, prayers, upright Christian morality—but in the sacraments they will have great additional treasures. Thus, the Catholic partners may address their Protestant spouses in these or similar terms: "I want these infinite treasures of faith handed on to our children, especially the real presence of Christ in the Holy Eucharist. That is the center of my life, and I cannot in good conscience deprive our children of it."

At the same time, the Catholic spouse should not try to pressure the other to enter the Catholic Church just for the sake of assuring the religious unity of the family. Protestants should join the Catholic Church only if they perceive that the Catholic faith possesses a fullness of truth and grace that their denomination does not, and if they discover the fundamental unity between the Church of the apostles and the Catholic Church.

Counseling Married Couples

As with marriage preparation, the priest must approach marital counseling with discernment and flexibility, since each couple is unique. Although we can give no general overview of this important service of the Church, we will take a look at two key topics—conflict resolution and the famous "midlife crisis"—and list a few common-sense recommendations for a good day in marriage.

1. Conflict Resolution

Conflicts and arguments occur in any healthy marital relationship. If the partners try to suppress their resentments, disagreements, and hurt feelings, this only aggravates the situation and might lead either to sudden irrational outbursts of anger or to a slow estrangement from each other. Priests should teach couples to face these tensions head on, but with patience, gentleness, and charity. When there is a conflict, it is important that they find the first opportunity—when they can talk in a calm, relaxed mood—to clear things up, reach an agreement, and, if needed, apologize to one other. I list here what I believe are the most important rules for couples to observe in solving a conflict situation:

- Avoid hurting each other's egos. Do not try to put down your spouse or undercut his or her self-esteem. Instead, explain what really hurts you. If you attack him or her, you are not only inviting a counterattack, but wounding yourself, your own flesh. Rather than putting down, explain gently but realistically what bothers you, and you will invite compassion and eagerness to help you.
- Never generalize. Do not say, for instance, "You always overspend" or "You are always late." Such generalizations invite self-defense and will make your complaint seem unrealistic.
- Never argue in the presence of others, especially your children. Children should always feel (and feel truthfully) that their parents are united. Even if the argument is not serious and does not threaten the marriage, children might develop anxiety if they overhear a heated exchange between their parents.
- Do not seek your parents' support for your side in an argument with your spouse. Your husband or wife will deeply resent this, sensing that you are still more attached to your parents than to him or her. Although there may be a few positive exceptions, in the case of parents who are mature enough to give impartial advice, this sort of intervention should typically be avoided.

- It may be helpful to agree in advance that during an argument you will hold hands. It is hard to get mad at your spouse as long as you are holding hands!

- If there is a blow-up, be the first to apologize (and apologize sincerely) rather than waiting for the other to be the first. Do not rationalize your resentful delay by thinking that your spouse "is more guilty than I am".

- Forgive and forget the incident. Do not nurture your past grievances, and do not use them as ammunition against your spouse in the next fight. If you do, he or she will rightly think, "You have never actually forgiven me." At the same time, "forgetting" is not the answer when there is a pattern of troubling behavior. If your spouse has a drinking problem or habitually overspends, for example, such habits need to be discussed, but in a loving way, without a condescending or vindictive attitude. Show your love and concern for your spouse rather than your (imagined) superiority.

2. Midlife Crisis

Most of us have seen marriages disintegrate unexpectedly after twenty or thirty years of apparently happy married life, with several children. The concrete reasons for these break-ups vary, but most derive from a midlife crisis, a spiritual and psychological phenomenon that affects both men and women, though in very different ways. We will start our discussion by reviewing the symptoms.

A typical man in a midlife crisis is dissatisfied with his life. He dreamed of a better career and hoped for greater satisfaction. What made him happy before now bores him. He might want to change jobs, but does not dare now, because he is afraid he will not find a better one. Professionally he feels stuck, and he takes out his frustrations, not on his boss, but on his family. Moreover, he feels a new surge of sexual desire, but his wife does not share his eagerness for frequent relations as she ages, especially with the onset of menopause. He may meet younger and more attractive women, whose charm he will struggle to resist. He begins to believe that he has the God-given and constitutionally assured right to pursue happiness, and that he will be happy if only he finds romantic love again. The man may even skew his memories of the past and conclude that he was never really happy with his wife. Attempting to find contentment before his life fades away, he ventures into extramarital escapades, or perhaps files for divorce and tries out a new marriage or partnership.

In women, the midlife crisis takes quite another form. Menopause, or the fear of it, makes a wife feel that she is no longer as beautiful and attractive as she was before. Also, she naturally feels less inclined to marital relations than in younger years, which may frustrate her husband and thus intensify her own sense of depreciation. With her children grown up and gone to college or living in their own homes, she and her husband—if they have not already developed a deep friendship—feel like two strangers living under the same roof, tense and nervous, with nothing left to share with each other. Without the duties of motherhood, she cannot figure out her role in the world. She feels lonely and used up in the empty house. Her temptation at this point may be to stir up her youthful charm and find a new man who, she thinks, better appreciates her beauty and personality.

Above, in the discussion on "Agreeing on a Plan for Marriage" during engagement, we listed some preventative measures that couples can take early on to avoid, or at least better handle, this kind of predicament. If the couple has put these into practice—and indeed, it is never too late to start—the crisis might be mild or even unnoticed. Here are a few additional suggestions for coping with the difficulties of a midlife crisis:

- The couple should feel safe admitting to each other what is really bothering them. If they have kept communicating throughout their marriage, this will come naturally. If not, this might be their last chance to confide in each other and make themselves vulnerable while asking for mutual help.
- The couple can soothe each other's bruised egos. The husband should assure his wife that she is still beautiful and attractive to him, and the wife should show her husband that she still admires him even though he has not been promoted or did not get the dream job he was hoping for.
- The wife can apply for a job if she did not have one before. This will help her to stay active once the children have moved away.

If the couple approaches the crisis in a positive way, they will certainly weather the storm, and their marriage will enter a new phase of security, deep love, and mutual support.

3. Recommendations for a Good Day in Marriage

Lastly, we offer some practical tips for living an ordinary day in marriage with love, joy, and fidelity.

- Alternate who prepares breakfast.
- Say at least a few kind words to each other in the morning.
- Kiss each other before you go your separate ways for the day.

- Call your spouse during the day. However, do not get into long stories if one of you has to get back to work.
- If you foresee that you will come home late, call your spouse. When it is your spouse who arrives late, however, do not start an interrogation session. Just be ready to listen to whatever he or she would like to share.
- Do not let your spouse do all the housework, even if you have been working all day. This is often a particular temptation for husbands. Ask about the day. Talk about the children. Do some cleaning. Help in the kitchen. However, if your spouse comes home tired after work and asks to be left alone, do not be offended or annoyed.
- Have a joyful family dinner at least several times a week, ideally when all the children are at table.
- Pray together before dinner, possibly spontaneously, voicing requests, praise, or thanksgiving.
- Relax and talk during meals. Be interested in what your children would like to tell you about their day.
- Husbands, if you want to make love that night, prepare your spouse emotionally, and do not insist if she is not well disposed.
- In lovemaking, be aware of each other's different needs. Focus on giving joy to your spouse.
- Time after a loving intercourse is very precious, especially for the wife. It is a time for conversation, for emotional and spiritual sharing.

CONTRACEPTION

Artificial contraception has become so widespread that many take it for granted, even seeing it as the responsible way to approach sex. Yet the Catholic Church has always taught that contraception—any disruption of the natural fertility of the sexual act—violates the dignity of human sexuality. Once cheap, effective contraceptives became widely available in the mid-twentieth century, especially the birth control pill, many Catholic couples, theologians, and priests began to believe that this magisterial teaching was due for a change. Thus when Pope Paul VI's 1968 encyclical *Humanae vitae* confirmed the Church's traditional stance—citing the immense dignity of sacramental love— many dissented, and many continue to dissent today.[5] How can priests approach the subject of contraception with both clarity and compassion?

First of all, we must ourselves be certain: the dissent of a number of theologians cannot invalidate a teaching of the Church, since the right to teach with authority belongs to the Magisterium (the pope and the bishops in union with him) and not to theologians. Popes John Paul II, Benedict XVI, and Francis have upheld, repeated, and deepened the teaching of *Humanae vitae*, and the bishops of the Catholic Church by and large support the Holy Father. For a more thorough account of the Catholic perspective on contraception, including responses to some common objections, see this book's appendix.

In contrast to the Church's teaching, there is a pervading mentality in the world that regards contraception as hardly more significant than cold medicine, and many priests either do not dare or simply do not want to teach against something so broadly accepted. As a result, a majority of Catholics still practice contraception today. Many argue that the use of contraception remains a matter of individual conscience. And in one sense, they are right: the Church has always taught that every moral imperative reaches us through our conscience, whose judgment

[5] A fuller account of this history is provided in the appendix.

is the proximate guide of moral action. Yet conscience does not create moral values and laws, but discovers them. Often, the false mentality of our environment—not to mention our own negligence—can obscure the "eye" of our conscience so that it becomes blind to certain real moral values, such as the rights of an oppressed ethnic minority, fidelity in marriage, or the integrity of the marital act. And while few would argue that such blindness can justify evil, it must be said that some couples who practice contraception do so in total ignorance. Priests must take this into account, and they must find tactful ways of educating the faithful. Yes, contraception is an objectively grave sin, but only God knows the extent of our *subjective* sin, of which we ourselves may be only vaguely aware.

If a person asks us about contraception in confession, we should not hesitate to explain what the Church teaches (see appendix), but always in a positive context. It is not enough to spell out clearly the natural moral law. The penitent must see that the purpose of the Church's insistence on the gravity of sexual sin is to protect the full dignity and beauty of the sexual act. She wants to preserve its power as a potential share in God's creative act and as a way of expressing true love, the total mutual gift of self, between husband and wife. Some may wonder why sex, if it is so powerful, needs guarding, and they must understand that because of our fallen human nature, we carry this treasure in a fragile vase. It easily shatters when misused, transforming into abuse—mutual or one-sided lust relief, frustration, and even torture. To use sex as God intended requires discipline and sacrifice, but this is simply the nature of the whole gospel, which entails a gradual and sometimes painful death to self in order to share more and more in the joy of Christ; there is no lasting love or joy without suffering.

Christian life presents a burden, but it is a light burden, since it is motivated by love.

In this context, a marriage that respects the integrity of the marital act becomes intelligible and attractive. Yet we find a paradox here: nobody can truly understand the reality of the teaching without practicing it. Only by living the Church's teaching on procreation can couples begin to trust and understand that by letting God be God in their lovemaking, they are opening their relationship to a new depth and purity. When abstaining from intercourse on fertile days to postpone or avoid pregnancy, the couple will find alternative ways to express affection. In this way, natural family planning (discussed in more detail in the appendix) can strengthen the romantic or emotional aspect of their relationship, and the couple can come to see that although intercourse may be the most dramatic form of intimacy, it is by no means the only one. A time of "courtship" with many signs of affection makes the sexual consummation all the more precious and appreciated. Moreover, if parents can abstain from sex for twelve or thirteen days a month, their encouragement of premarital chastity will sound all the more convincing to their teenagers.

Indissolubility of Marriage

According to Catholic teaching, a sacramental marriage that has been physically consummated cannot be dissolved by any authority whatsoever. If God has joined a couple together in the Sacrament of Marriage and they have become one flesh, they remain for life husband and wife. Their marriage bond shares in the indissoluble bond that unites Christ and the Church; thus, they can always count on the healing, forgiving presence of Christ in their marriage, provided that they are open to it.

1. Separation and Civil Divorce

If one or both partners fail in a sacramental marriage, a situation may arise in which the partners poison and destroy each other's lives and those of their children as well. If, for instance, one of the partners becomes an alcoholic or verbally or physically abusive or simply refuses to give up an extramarital liaison, separation may be not only justified but also necessary. A civil divorce may follow to assure the financial security of all concerned. Yet even after a civil divorce, the couple remains married in the eyes of God. At least the partner who is more open to God's grace should not stop praying, interceding for his or her marriage partner so that God may give this person the grace of conversion. Not only is an unconditionally loving marriage partner who remains faithful a powerful image of Christ, Who is faithful to us even if we turn our backs on Him, but his or her prayer may become the God-given means eventually to save the unfaithful spouse.

2. Annulment

Annulment is an official declaration of the Church that what appeared to be a marriage lacked from its inception one of the essential ingredients of a sacramental marriage and, therefore, was nonexistent from the beginning. In spite of the built-in imperfections of the annulment process, its declarations of nullity have helped to lift unnecessary burdens from many consciences. Annulment of the marriage is declared if one or more ingredients of a valid marriage are missing. The essential (minimal) ingredients of marriage are the following:

1. Sufficient maturity to be aware of the responsibilities of marriage. Thus, lack of due discretion is a cause for annulment.
2. Right intention: to remain faithful to each other until death and give each other the right to have children.[6] Thus, if one of the partners reserved the right to divorce or the right to extramarital affairs, the marriage is invalid.
3. The physical ability to perform sexual intercourse. However, only permanent impotence, not sterility, makes the marriage invalid.
4. The psychological ability to live as husband and wife. For instance, serious sociopathy (inability to live in an intimate relationship) does render a marriage invalid. If the couple could not live as husband or wife, the marriage never came into being.
5. The canonical form of the marriage (in the presence of a Catholic priest duly delegated for the wedding), unless the couple received dispensation from it. Thus, a Catholic who, without asking for a dispensation, attempts marriage in a Protestant church does not receive the Sacrament of Marriage.

Normally, the annulment process starts with a consultation with the parish priest. If his response is inadequate, the person should get in touch with the marriage counseling office or marriage tribunal of the diocese.

3. Divorced and Remarried Catholics

Catholics in a second marriage without previous annulment often come to us with the desire to return to the

---

[6] The use of contraception is opposed by the Church, but its use does not in itself make the marriage invalid unless one partner excludes even the right of the other to have children.

sacraments. If we see probable causes for annulment, we should recommend that they initiate the process either through us or through a pastor who can help them collect the necessary information and fill out the application form. We must also explain to them why they should abstain from sexual relations until they receive the decree of annulment.

If the first marriage, however, is ascertained to be a sacramental, consummated marriage, the priest faces a very delicate and possibly long-lasting task. He should explain to the petitioning spouse the reasons why the first marriage is sacred and indissoluble by any earthly authority. In the Sacrament of Marriage, the couple asked Jesus Christ that they may share in the bond which unites Christ with His Bride the Church, and this bond is unbreakable. Christ will never abandon His Church, so the spouses whom Christ has joined together cannot break the sacramental bond that has united them. If no reconciliation and reunion is possible, the party who intends to live a Christian life should pray for the other spouse. Such prayers coming from a suffering heart might save the other party.

If, after the break-up of a sacramental marriage, a Catholic attempts remarriage civilly or in a non-Catholic Christian ceremony, the new marriage is invalid in the eyes of the Church. If a remarried couple wants to share fully in the sacramental life of the Church, they should separate, unless the good of their children calls for continuing to live together. If they promise to live together as brother and sister, they may be absolved and admitted to Holy Communion, even if future lapses might be foreseen; the Sacrament of Reconciliation will help them to start all over again.

Pope Francis' post-synodal apostolic exhortation *Amoris laetitia* goes one controversial step further. It explains that there are people living in an ecclesiastically invalid second marriage who would like to share in the sacramental life of the Church but feel that living as brother and sister is practically impossible. Separation may not be feasible either for various reasons: it might cause the children to grow up without a father or mother, or without necessary financial support. Pope Francis writes: "Because of forms of conditioning and mitigating factors, it is possible that in an objective situation of sin—which may not be subjectively culpable, or fully such—a person can be living in God's grace, can love and can also grow in the life of grace and charity, while receiving the Church's help to this end. Discernment must help to find possible ways of responding to God and growing in the midst of limits."[7] The famous footnote 351 of *Amoris laetitia* for such cases has this to say: "In certain cases, this can include the help of the sacraments. Hence, 'I want to remind priests that the confessional must not be a torture chamber, but rather an encounter with the Lord's mercy' (Apostolic Exhortation *Evangelii Gaudium* [24 November 2013], 44: AAS 105 [2013], 1038). I would also point out that the Eucharist 'is not a prize for the perfect, but a powerful medicine and nourishment for the weak' (*ibid.*, 47: 1039)." The pope is not saying that anyone in a subjective state of mortal sin may be allowed to receive Holy Communion. That would indeed be heretical, clearly contrary to the Catholic faith. Rather, he recognizes, and rightly so, that there are people who are objectively in the state of grave sin, such as an invalid marital union, and yet are not subjectively guilty of mortal sin.

How are we to put the teaching of *Amoris laetitia* into practice? I, along with many bishops and theologians, believe that admission to the sacraments without a sincere promise

[7] No. 305.

of a brother-sister relationship—even though dogmatically possible—should not be allowed, for grave pastoral reasons. A false impression has spread among the faithful that indissolubility is only an ideal and not a binding obligation of sacramental marriage, and we must not let it take deeper root. Such practices have already caused, and will continue to cause, disunity in the Church, setting one bishop against the other, as well as one bishops' conference against another. At the same time, however, we need to take seriously the injunction of *Amoris laetitia* that we should accompany these couples with the greatest love and understanding, treat them as members of the Church, and involve them in her life. We should ask them to pray and to trust that God will give them the grace to fulfill His will and will bear them up with a father's love in their struggle.

SAME-SEX ATTRACTION

As we discussed in the previous chapter, those who counsel people with same-sex attraction—whether the counseling takes place inside or outside of confession—need to express both natural respect for them as God's children and an understanding of and commitment to the truth of the Catholic teaching on sexuality. Only a priest with genuine compassion and a firm trust in the Church's teaching can truly guide and console people with homosexual attraction.

There is much controversy about the causes of same-sex attraction: whether it is genetic or due to environmental factors. Priests should stay out of this discussion since it lies outside their field of competence and is irrelevant to their task. Regardless of the cause, the Catholic Church, based on the Bible and her tradition, has always taught that consent to homosexual relations in will or in action is gravely sinful but that same-sex attraction is not, since the person is not responsible for it. We must unpack both of these teachings to understand the fullness of the Catholic perspective.

Firstly, the Old and New Testaments could not be clearer in their teaching on homosexual activity. In the Letter to the Romans, Saint Paul describes such acts as the result of man's rejection of the true God and his turning to idols (Rom 1:18–28; see also 1 Cor 6:9–10). Just as idolaters rejected the true God and created their own idols, so do homosexual acts invert God's order of creation. Those who engage in them live out their own desires in contradiction to God's law, which is inscribed in their bodies. The male and female bodies are designed for heterosexual relations in which husband and wife become one flesh. In a real sense, they are able to enter into each other's bodies, which also invites them to be in one another spiritually by mutual self-giving love. Their union is life giving, not only biologically, but metaphysically, since God, the author of life, wills the husband and wife to be "partners" with Him through their loving union. The same-sex couple, on the other hand, can never really become one; the same sexual organs cannot be "fitted" into each other, and anal sex and mutual masturbation can hardly be called union. Moreover, though a homosexual couple may love one another as friends, homosexual activity does not give life. To any kind of propaganda that insists on the equal value of homo- and heterosexual sex, Christians should react kindly but firmly.[8]

---

[8] We can also tell persons with homosexual attraction about some reputable psychologists and psychiatrists who claim that with professional help many of them may develop an ability for lasting heterosexual relationships, even if the same-sex desire might remain as a strong temptation. See, for example,

At the same time, the phenomenon of same-sex attraction, even among prayerful, virtuous people, cannot be denied. Indeed, after reading the previous paragraph, a homosexually attracted person might well respond in frustration, "But why did God create this contradiction? I cannot help what I desire, and what I desire—you say—goes against the order of creation and cannot be fulfilled. This God is either cruel or nonexistent!" How can we answer him? God indeed allows natural processes, for various reasons, to fail. Yet His almighty love can turn any disorder or hurtful effect into a blessing. Homosexual desire gives a providential opportunity for a Christian to learn to become the master rather than the slave of his desires and to redirect his sexual energies toward good activities. Struggles of this kind are a part of human life. Most people are beset with various weaknesses and face similar (but perhaps not so heroic) challenges in other areas. Take the example of an aggressive person. He will never become passive and inactive, and he has to work to hold back his outbursts. But he has the choice between becoming a ruthless tyrant—the more automatic tendency—or growing into an effective, benevolent leader. So persons with same-sex attraction, too, can choose to channel their desires. Many of them have a natural inclination to be personable, kind, sensitive, and helpful, and they can become particularly good friends, contributors, volunteers, and community leaders. They have a great capacity for love—a love that homosexual activity would simply compromise. To use a friend's body to satisfy my lust degrades him or

the website of the Catholic Medical Association's resources on this issue: *Homosexuality and Hope*. There are other professionals who declare that any effort to change sexual orientation is impossible or even harmful. No matter who is right, the harassment and ridicule by some gay activists of those who claim that change is possible is deplorable.

her, whether or not the act is consensual. A chaste friendship loves the bodily and personal integrity of the friend,
desires the growth and flourishing of the other. Reverence
and distance are conditions for true intimacy.

During His earthly ministry, Christ always had a "preferential love" for those sinners whom the self-righteous
scorned and rejected. Thus, as said before, *respect and compassion (rather than condescension and disgust) are essential in the
attitude of the priest* when dealing with same-sex attracted
Christians. According to the assessment of the Catholic
Medical Association's surveys, active homosexual people
typically have low self-esteem, whether or not they admit
it to themselves, and this self-loathing often leads them
to alcoholism or suicide. The Church must not abandon
these people or allow them to be driven away by unchar-
ity. Priests should point out to their people how false, sinful, and un-Christian any form of "gay bashing" is and ask
them to welcome any gay or lesbian person with love into
the church community, yet without creating any ambigu-
ity regarding the Church's teaching. The Church's support
for these people should also extend to the environment in
which they live: families, schools, and society at large. Let
me mention briefly a few important issues. Parents should
provide a warm, loving family atmosphere in which the
children are appreciated for who they are rather than for
their talents and achievements. They should remain close
to their children, and the fathers should spend time and talk
with their teenagers. Both girls and boys need for various
reasons the reassuring and attractive presence of both father
and mother.[9] At the same time, parents should not cling
to the children for their own emotional needs, but instead

[9] In the case of a same-sex couple, the child needs the close presence of a role
model of his or her own sex.

allow them to grow up. In school, teachers should not simply communicate knowledge but also care personally for their students, help them to include and accept everyone in the class, and ban any homosexual joke or bullying.

We should tell these poor ones the truth: Christ is closer to them in their poverty than to many other people, knocking at the door and asking to be admitted into their lives and into their souls. Their condition of same-sex attraction might be that point of weakness where they become vulnerable enough to receive the intimations of divine love. "For when I am weak," says Saint Paul, "then I am strong" (2 Cor 12:10). Homosexually attracted people are called to holiness just as everybody else is, except that their condition attracts God's special love and concern for them. The Lord's special love, however, calls for a special response. They must carry a particular load, and their struggle for chastity will demand real effort. But He who gave them this distinctive burden will also give them—if they truly ask for it—the grace to turn the burden into a blessing. Loneliness is hard to endure, but if accepted out of love for Christ, it will become a means of chaste intimacy. Unchaste behavior—both heterosexual and homosexual—destroys the truth and joy of relationships. Just as celibate heterosexuals can channel (or "sublimate") their sexual energies into chaste celibate friendships, so too can homosexual people. The chaste gay or lesbian person is called to be "a sign that will be contradicted" by the culture, ridiculed and perhaps ostracized. Yet their prayers, serenity, joy, and loving openness will help many others to see that God's law is good and rejuvenates the heart.

The implicit conviction of our culture is that there can be no real happiness without sexual fulfillment. Millions of Catholic priests and religious across the centuries, especially the saints, have proven that this is utterly false, but their testimony does not count for much in our age. If psychologists do not believe in the peace and joy of millions of Catholic celibates, then let them ask the much larger group of Hindu and Buddhist celibate monks. They give witness to the same: man can flourish without sexual fulfillment, but he cannot flourish without friendship. In this regard, I feel that homosexuals have, in a certain sense, a built-in advantage. Yes, their condition comes with a heavy cross, but each human being has his own cross. The acceptance of any cross with faith and love in God helps us deepen and ennoble our humanity and, in the long run, our crosses will turn into blessings.

CHAPTER 8

Suffering, Dying, and the Anointing of the Sick

One of the most frequent questions—if not *the* most frequent—a priest has to deal with is the question of evil and, more concretely, of suffering. People understand that evil men and women deserve suffering as a just punishment, but there are so many innocent children who suffer and many adults whose suffering seems absurd, a cruel torture by blind fate. If a priest has not suffered or has not been close to suffering people, he will not be able to give a credible answer. C. S. Lewis wrote a beautiful book on the problem of evil before the agony and death of his wife, but only after it occurred did he become truly able to empathize with the suffering and dying.

A theologian might respond: there was no death or pain in God's original plan of creation. The sin of our ancestors brought suffering and dying into the world and started an avalanche of personal and collective sins, which God allowed for the sake of a greater good. This answer is true on the level of theory. But without understanding the nature of sin and its "natural" consequences, this explanation does not make sense to most people.

The sin of our ancestors was the attempt "to become like gods" by eating of the forbidden fruit. God intended to give them a share in His own divine life, but they wanted to grab it on their own, rather than receive it as a gift from

God. Ever since, every sin is a repeat performance of putting oneself above God by setting one's own will above
God's will. For instance, "I know God has forbidden adultery, but today I've decided that it will be better for me
to yield to my craving for this woman than to go home
and put up with the endless nagging of my wife." Thus
sin is always an attempt to become my own god and turn
away from the true God. But God is the "living God",
the source of all life, so the sinner disrupts his own lifeline:
friendship with God. The result is obviously suffering and
death. Most likely, if man had not sinned, he would have
had only to "cross over" from a biological life, in which
he had to choose between God and sin, into eternal life
of communion with God. Perhaps it would have been a
peaceful *dormitio*, a falling asleep, just as Mary passed from
this world into God's eternity. Our present suffering and
dying, then, is the result of sin, the necessary consequence
of distancing oneself from God, the source of all life. It is
both a punishment and a way of healing, a tunnel that may
lead to eternal life or eternal death.

Out of the Father and Son's common decision, Jesus
came among us as a man, not to give lectures on the phi-
losophy of suffering, but to take upon Himself all our sins
and their consequences: suffering and dying. He suffered
and died the sinner's death, our death. In His Incarnation,
life, and agony, God showed to each one of us, who desire
to live like gods, how to accept our creaturely condition
and accept our dying as expiation for our sins in obedience, trust, and love.

The priest's job, then, is to encourage and help suffering
or dying persons to unite their ordeal with the life-giving
suffering and death of Christ. When people learn that they
have a terminal disease and will shortly die, this may be
the jolt they need to wake up from a life of self-deception.
They must admit to themselves that they are not immortal

gods, but instead creatures whose lives hang on a thin thread and will soon fade away. They may then develop a new outlook on their past lives, their successes and failures, what they have done and what they have neglected. They may realize how many chances they missed to love those whom God gave them to love, and how much energy and effort they wasted on useless things. This discovery may be followed by a sincere repentance and the desire to use well the time left for them. They may renew and deepen their love for their family and friends and make up for hurts and offenses they have caused. As their pain grows and as they experience the gradual deterioration of their bodies, the fear of total annihilation will intensify. The challenge, then, is to trust and love God in this situation when they feel most forsaken by Him. It is by facing this challenge that they may come closest to Christ, Who took upon Himself our death and shared the agony of our dying. At the end, the most terrifying reality, death, may turn into a blessing for us: it may become a powerful "therapy" that brings us back to reality and self-knowledge, to loving others and to trusting and loving God.

However, this process of "reality-therapy" is not smooth and certainly not automatic. Dying persons need the help of their families, their friends, and the Church to make sense of the terrible things that are happening to them. Normally, a dying patient goes through psychological stages in reacting to his death. The first stage is disbelief: when someone hears the bad news, he often does not believe it. He thinks it may have been a misdiagnosis and therefore seeks alternative opinions. After the inevitability of death has sunk in, the patient rebels: "Why do I have to die? Why not these older friends of mine or why not this or that person who sinned so much more than I have?" Once he has passed the stage of rebellion, he will bargain for time. "If I could go home only one more time, sit on my porch, and enjoy the sunset", said one patient with liver cancer when he could not even sit up in bed. Finally, there comes acceptance, and if the patient has faith, it will be an acceptance with trust in God's mercy and love.

We can also tell sick and dying people with faith that this might be the most important and most helpful stage of their lives. If they offer their sufferings and unite them with Christ's, they can effectively help others for whom they ask God's favor. The Father loves and takes most seriously the intercession of His children for their neighbors.

The Role of Family and Friends

Family and friends should make themselves available to the patient. Rather than trying to prolong "a fool's paradise" for themselves and for the patient by avoiding the dreaded closeness of dying, they should be willing to listen when the patient wants to talk about his pain and anxiety. They can only do this if they have accepted their own death at least in some initial way. Moreover, instead of being afraid to share the patient's feelings of fear and despair, family and friends should show their closeness to the patient by physical signs of care and love, holding his hand, kissing, and hugging. Only if they accept solidarity with the patient in this way can they help him in the challenge of trusting and loving God. Finally, if the patient is Catholic, family and friends should encourage him to receive the Sacrament of the Anointing of the Sick.

Anointing of the Sick

The following are the essential words of imparting the sacrament as the priest anoints the patient's head and hands:

"Through this holy anointing may the Lord in his love and mercy help you with the grace of the Holy Spirit. May the Lord who frees you from sin save you and raise you up." It is important to teach our people that this sacrament is not just for the terminally ill, but for anyone who is seriously sick and even for elderly people simply suffering the debilitating effects of old age. If received in faith, the sacrament unites the sick person with the suffering Christ so that with Him he may conquer his illness. Overwhelmed by pain and fever, sick people are tempted to think only of themselves, concentrating on their pain, forgetting about God and other people. The sacrament helps them overcome this lethargy and raises them up so that they anticipate their resurrected life by renewing their trust, developing their courage to suffer in union with Christ.

Oftentimes, a visible alleviation follows the anointing, and at times even bodily healing. We could explain such healings this way: the sacrament restores or deepens peace with God and with one's fellow men and provides a source of spiritual energy. The peace and strength of the soul can strengthen the natural processes of the body to overcome the disease.[1] However, this is exceptional. If the person is dying, the sacrament helps him to unite himself with the dying of Christ.

SPEAKING TO THE TERMINALLY ILL

The question often arises: Should the relatives or doctors tell the patient that he is terminally ill? Every patient has the right to know the truth about his condition. By lying

[1] Modern medicine takes more and more seriously the psychosomatic unity of man, and acknowledges that the "state of the soul" of a patient often determines how successful a medical treatment is.

or by silence, one deprives the sick person of an opportunity to prepare for the final encounter with God. Still, as long as there is hope for recovery, we should strengthen the patient's hope, since recovery depends also on the sick person's inner disposition. But if there is no hope, the truth must be told with tact and love. Some doctors declare the terminal condition in an abrupt, matter-of-fact way and leave the room before the patients can ask any questions: "How soon? How much pain? How will it happen?" The doctor should assure them that he remains available to the dying person, as well as assure them about the many ways the pain can be alleviated. If this task of telling the truth falls to members of the family, they should act in a similar way, reassuring the dying person of their love and closeness.

EUTHANASIA

Etymologically, "euthanasia" means "dying well", but the current meaning of the word is the painless termination of a human life, either by a positive act (for example, a lethal injection) or by withholding ordinary means of medical care. Even though euthanasia is still illegal in many civilized countries, it has supporters everywhere who are determined to change the law. They advocate abortion for mentally or physically handicapped babies and euthanasia for the terminally ill and for those in great pain who can no longer enjoy life. They claim that a civilized country should provide a chance for everyone to "die with dignity" rather than force both patient and relatives to go through a long agony.

The Catholic Church and many other Christian churches consider direct euthanasia morally wrong, since God alone is the Lord and giver of life. We do not own our lives; rather, we have to account for what we have done with them. This does not, however, preclude using drugs to ease or eliminate pain, even if their side effect is to accelerate the death of a terminally ill patient.

The Catholic Church also teaches that one is not obligated to use extreme measures to prolong life. Life on earth is a great value, but not an absolute value to which one should cling at all costs. If there is no hope of recovery, the patient or the next of kin may give permission to turn off the life-support system. Nor is one obligated to undergo a very risky surgery whose benefits are questionable. There is a clear distinction between terminating the life of someone and letting someone die by not using radical means to keep him alive. But in practice, the increasing availability of ever-new technologies blurs this distinction and makes it difficult to decide how far one should go in prolonging life. Of course, whether or not a treatment is an extreme measure (in technical terms, "extraordinary means") depends on many factors. For instance, a heart bypass procedure, routinely performed in the United States and not considered extraordinary for the average patient, would be considered extraordinary treatment in many countries. What would be a low-risk surgery for a younger patient could be an extreme measure for an elderly person.

In general, whether or not a treatment is extraordinary in a given situation for a given individual should be decided according to (1) how much hope it offers for recovery or for meaningful prolongation of life; (2) how much pain it requires the patient to undergo; and (3) how much of a financial burden it will be. For instance, a person might refuse chemotherapy if it would only prolong his agony and exhaust the family's savings. Allowing a person to die by discontinuing or not applying the use of extreme measures is sometimes called "passive euthanasia".

When talking with a dying person who would like to commit assisted suicide, we could explain that the last days, weeks, or months could be the most important time in his life. God will meet us in the shape and form we have attained at the last conscious moment of our life. Existentialist philosophers are partially right in claiming that man is free to create himself. Obviously, the range of choices is limited by hereditary and environmental factors, but it is still a real freedom. Cooperating with the Holy Spirit, we can expand our hearts to receive the Father's love that makes us His children, brothers and sisters of Christ. But we can also freely reject God's grace up to the very end of our life and then arrive at the end unable to love, finding eternity a *mors immortalis*, an undying death, in the words of Saint Bernard. If a person forgoes euthanasia, the last act of a self-destructing freedom, he will have time to regret a loveless life and to long for God's forgiveness. If until now he has had only a mediocre, lukewarm love for God and men, he now has the chance to let God purify and perfect his love. Only God knows how much time we need on earth to be ready to meet Him.

SUICIDE

By discussing euthanasia, we have already established the principles that need to be applied to the morality of suicide. Since our life is God's gift, a gift we do not own, we cannot simply discard it. By killing themselves, suicide victims imply: "It is better for me to die than to live. God's gift is of no value to me. I don't trust that this situation will turn out for my good." Yet Christ's Cross reveals to us how the worst suffering became the greatest treasure of all humankind. If Christians unite themselves with Christ and offer their sufferings for others, their lives, no matter how humiliating and painful, become life giving for others.

Because of the sin involved, people who lose loved ones to suicide suffer a terrible, traumatic blow. They worry about the soul of the deceased, and they may even hold themselves responsible, asking themselves why they did not do more. We priests must have great compassion for those who are touched by suicide. Although we know that suicide is objectively a grave sin, we should not presume that suicide victims are responsible for killing themselves. Rather, we must explain to their relatives what modern psychology has shown: in the great majority of cases, the person who commits or attempts suicide has a mental disorder (irrational fear, severe depression, hallucinations) that diminishes or takes away moral responsibility. For this reason, the Church today does not deny a Church burial to suicide victims.

CHAPTER 9

Guiding Children and Adolescents

In my younger years, a fashionable theory prevailed in some elite catechetical circles: we priests should focus on educating the parents and then let the parents educate their children. Clearly, adult formation is an important task in every parish and in every Catholic school, but children and adolescents must also benefit from direct contact with priests. Modern psychology makes it abundantly clear that a child's first impressions have a decisive impact on the rest of his life. The child's first contact with priests should show him Jesus' preferential love for children, as well as His joy and interest in them.

Time spent teaching children about God and His kingdom does not by any means go down the drain. In fact, religion teachers of little children are often amazed by how lively and inexhaustible children's interest is in the life of heaven. They have not yet sinned in any serious way, and so it is evident to them that God wants their happiness and that He does not want them to die but to remain close to Him. Parents play a pivotal role here. In a home in which father and mother both love the children and love and trust each other, children indeed experience a foretaste of heaven, and the memory of such a home will greatly influence their own adult relationships, even if they drift from the faith.

We have already seen, in chapter 6, how a confessor can work with children and—more complexly—with adolescents. We have also compiled some dating and "pre-dating" advice for teenagers in chapter 7, which priests can use in counseling and spiritual direction. In this short discussion, we will focus instead on helping parents to raise their kids with love, joy, and truth, especially during the troubled adolescent years.

Love your teenagers for their own sake rather than for your own vicarious satisfaction.

This is the single most important guideline for parents in general but especially for parents of teenagers, who begin to look with critical eyes at their parents. Even if the parents hardly ever verbalize the real reason for their satisfaction or disappointment with their teenagers, an adolescent can sense by his parents' body language how they feel about him. If parents only give affection and praise when their child is successful academically, athletically, or socially, their teenagers sense that they are not really loved. They believe that their parents love them only because they are a "credit to them". A father may feel vicarious satisfaction if one of his sons is a formidable football player, praising him while at the same time looking down on his other son who excels in mathematics rather than athletics. With other parents, of course, the situation might be reversed. The father loves the mathematically excellent son, but does not notice the athletic talents of the other, whom he is always ready to scold. Mothers are usually more person-oriented, yet some of them also show or withhold affection on the basis of their children's talents.

In this context, we see why mentally or physically challenged children may become a great blessing for a family.

If the couple is not ashamed of them but instead embraces them with great love and care, the other, healthy children will learn this unconditional love from their parents. This, then, is the paradox: those who are often looked upon by the world as second-rate humans may become a great humanizing force in the family.

Have time, understanding, and respect for your teenager.

The adolescent years of children are indeed the most difficult challenge for parents in general. On certain days, teenagers withdraw and seek to distance themselves from their parents, while on other days they look for opportunities to communicate. This requires from the parents a great deal of tact in giving enough space to their sons and daughters, but it also requires that the parents remain available to talk and spend time with the kids when they need it. Sons, whether they admit it or not, usually love to do "manly" things with their fathers, such as hunting, hiking, and other sports, which all provide great opportunities for a good man-to-man talk between father and son. Girls also need opportunities to spend time and talk with their father. After all, he is the first male they come to know, and a good father-daughter relationship will have an impact on what kind of boyfriends the girl will choose, as well as how she will relate to them. Similarly, the close, affectionate, but not oppressive relationship of male and female teenagers to their mother is crucial for the warmth and health of their later relationships.

If we consider these needs of teenagers, we understand why so many in this vulnerable age group go astray and take many years—if not their entire lives—to reach a state of mature adulthood. Absent, tired, emotionally distant parents try to make up for the lack of a warm, cheerful, and intimate home by fulfilling every whim of their sons and daughters; yet these same parents are surprised that their children dislike being at home and remain distant from them. Parents often treat their teenagers as if they were still little children, a misperception that can lead to tension and mutual resentment or, in the case of passive and spoiled adolescents, even to arrested emotional development. The latter always aim to please but are afraid to make even small independent decisions, while stronger and more aggressive characters rebel and create turmoil in the family. The antidote to this is *respect*. Such respect entails both discipline and freedom, justice and mercy, honesty and kindness.

I quote here the words of a loving father to his teenage son, words that would have a great positive influence on the son's future: "You are getting into a difficult stage in your life. Your moods will roller coaster up and down, from elation to depression, from anger and frustration to regret and shame. You may find our rules sometimes unreasonable or ridiculous, my attitude and your mother's old-fashioned and out of date. Regardless, we expect you to obey us. But you should know that we will understand you and forgive you." Recognizing his father's sincerity, the teenager was impressed. He felt understood, accepted, and yet put on notice of what was expected of him. He grew up without ever causing headaches for his parents.

Set up reasonable rules and stick to them.

Teenagers will argue about rules and curfews; they will try to bend and circumvent them. Nevertheless, they will feel secure and confident if they know that their parents accept responsibility for guiding them.

Parents should tell their teenagers that they would very much like to trust them. If sons and daughters want more freedom, they should prove by their actions that they are worthy of trust.

The most powerful weapon spoiled teenagers have over their parents is the withdrawal of affection if the parents dare to say no to them. By many subtle or not-so-subtle signs, these teenagers may try to show that the parents, who "don't understand", have become unworthy of the teenagers' affection. If the parents are insecure, they will capitulate; in spite of their own better judgment, they will yield to their teenagers' pressure. Although the teenagers might feel triumphant for a moment, in the long run their respect for their parents will diminish. The teenagers might even feel disappointed when they discover that their parents are so weak that they can be easily manipulated.

Find ways to compliment your teens, but also dare to criticize them.

Regardless of what they say, teenagers highly value their parents' opinion. It can be a great motivating force if they receive a compliment that they feel is honest and well deserved. Their talents should be acknowledged with gratitude but not exaggerated. A child should be happy and grateful for the talents he has received, but if he comes to look down on those he believes to be less talented, he deceives himself by claiming credit for what is a pure gift from God. He should have a healthy pride in, and gratitude for, what he has done with his talents. Again, the child should not ever feel that his parents' love depends upon his skills, achievements, or personality.

Unconditional love does not mean undemanding love. If parents love their children, they will demand that they become their very best. If the teenager fails in something through his own fault, perhaps even a serious moral transgression, they need to help him to own up to his failure and regret it. Yet parents must always forgive their child and offer him new chances to prove and improve himself. Therefore, a parent should never say, "I don't forgive you" or "I disown you." Such statements reveal that the parent's love was always conditional, that is, it depended on the credit the child may have brought to his parents.

Sex education is primarily the duty of parents.

Very few parents have the courage to face up to the task of gradually introducing to their children the mysteries of sexual relations and the origin of human life. The result will naturally be a restless curiosity that seeks enlightenment from smart phones and from other children or teens. Realizing that adults do not dare to speak about these matters, adolescents become excited about their alleged knowledge of the forbidden fruit, and they begin to engage in secret experimentation. The parents usually realize what is happening only when it is too late: their son, sometimes at eleven or twelve, is already addicted to pornography. By the time such a boy begins to date, his experience of sex is already warped; not only does the lust of the flesh rule his imagination and intrude itself into normal boy-girl relationships, but he grows detached from *real* women, preferring the illusory company of strangers he will never meet, who reveal themselves on screen with a simulated love.

The ideal place for sex education is the family, and its program should follow the physiological and psychological development of the child. However, since very few parents feel competent to teach children about sex, the task often falls upon teachers and at times also upon priests. Parents should not shirk the responsibility. It is essential

that parents explain the meaning of sexual union respectfully and gradually, making sure not to feed the child
any fairy tales, the falsehood of which, when discovered,
will diminish the child's trust in his parents. The parents'
explanation should precede the "enlightening" efforts of
peers. At a certain age, little children become very interested in where they were before they were born. Parents
can awaken a sense of wonder and love in their children
by explaining to them that God was thinking about them
and then created them. God created them because He
loved them, and therefore He blessed the loving union
of husband and wife so that they might bring a baby into
the world. I recommend the following beautiful answer
that a mother gave to her child about where he was before
birth: "You were under my heart. I carried you there for
nine months." If the parents treat questions on sexuality
as a secret taboo, it only stirs up the child's eager curiosity. No question should be left without a true answer, yet
an answer proportionate to the child's development. If
we speak about sex matter-of-factly, explaining its great
dignity as a creative cooperation with God, children and
adolescents will be less susceptible to the corrupting influence of a secular environment.

The only parents successful in "sex education" are those
who have themselves fought the good fight and have
managed to integrate their sexual drive, personal love, and
enduring commitment into their lives. These parents can
speak credibly and respectfully about sexual development,
dating, and marriage. They can also awaken the sense of a
sacred mystery as they talk about the generation and birth
of children. They will explain the source of the sacredness of
sexual intercourse, the potentially creative presence of God
in the act, and the "partnership" of the couple with Him
in bringing forth a new human being. Adolescents who

receive such formation will no longer burn with a morbid curiosity and will be able to speak openly and respectfully about sexual matters.

Make sure to have at least some "family meals" each week, as well as conversation during these meals.

This traditional feature of family living is becoming more and more difficult to maintain. Every one of the children has different activities scheduled for almost every evening, one of the parents may come home late after dinnertime, and everyone is in a hurry because they do not want to miss out on anything in their crowded agenda. Yet some families manage the seemingly impossible and have family meals together at least on certain days of the week. If both father and mother look forward to them, they can put a wholesome limit on sports, piano lessons, and parties so that the family can enjoy time together. If the parents enjoy each other's company, chances are that even their teenagers will open up, tell their stories, and resist the urge to run out on the rest of the family.

Talk with your children about religious issues, and take them to church.

A child learns about the world from his parents. Through the parents' faith, the child learns about God and His role in our lives. If the parents' faith is real—something more than social façade or mere habit—then the child will instinctively know that he shares in something authentic and valuable. If the parents pay only lip service to Christianity, the children will become spiritually deprived, "undernourished" in matters of the soul. Sooner or later they will sense the lie behind the parents' words or observe the contradiction between their words and lives. When such children reach adolescence, they will very likely face a serious crisis of faith.

However, even teenagers of a sincerely Christian family may endure a period of doubt and confusion, after taking their faith for granted in childhood. Typically, the crisis comes when adolescents begin to probe the knowledge and the way of life of their parents. They associate their childhood thinking and acting with immaturity and dependence and want to grow out of it. If they find no opportunity for a deeper understanding of their faith that makes sense to them and responds to their questions, they might reject Christianity along with their childhood.

Parents who have an adult understanding of their faith can be of great help. They will be able to point out their own reasons for believing and answer the objections of their children. They will show how their faith helped them turn the crises of their lives into opportunities to grow in strength and goodness. If the children sense their parents' sincerity and experience the joys and peace of a loving home, sooner or later most of them will long to tap into the mysterious source of their parents' goodness.

If the teenagers insist that they neither want to pray nor go to Mass because of their doubts, the parents can respond: "Would you stop speaking to us and regarding us as your parents just because you had doubts about it? Would you disown your dad because you don't have DNA evidence of paternity? Would you not wait to make any serious decision until you found out the truth? God says He is our Father. Would you stop talking and praying to Him just because you have some doubts? Do you see that you would be justified in disregarding Him as a product of your imagination only if you became *convinced* of His nonexistence? For our family, the Sunday Mass is the most important time of the week; Christ Himself is waiting for us there. As long as you live with us, we want you to come with us. You can always imitate the prayer of the father who brought his sick boy to Jesus, saying, 'I believe; help my unbelief!' (Mk 9:24)."

The reality of God's kingdom can be tested, too, by discerning the fruits of our actions. Any time we obey God's word and act upon it, we have more peace and goodness in our souls. Conversely, we see that disobedience to God's word proves this in a negative way: inner peace and goodness fade away as soon as we ignore the word of God. Teenagers can be taught to recognize the Lord in the discernment of spirits.

CHAPTER 10

Spiritual Guidance
and Direction

We have talked implicitly about spiritual guidance in every chapter of this book by discussing the priest's prayer life, his virtues, and his ways of preaching, teaching, and celebrating the sacraments. All these activities serve either directly or indirectly the way he guides souls to God. In prayer, the priest lifts souls up to God; by his virtues, he gives the faithful a living example of following Christ; and through the ministry of the Word and sacraments, he enables his flock's direct transforming encounter with Jesus Christ. However, there still remain a few issues that need to be addressed.

In principle, any priest, religious brother, or layman, as well as any woman, lay or religious, may become a trustworthy spiritual guide, since the administration of the sacraments is not the guide's fundamental task. Obtaining an academic degree in spiritual direction may be helpful, but it is neither a necessary nor a sufficient qualification for the job. Here I can only outline the most important personal qualities, those natural and supernatural charisms that the early Fathers thought were necessary for the *technê technôn kai epistême epistêmôn* ("the art of arts and the science of sciences").

Discernment of Spirits

The goal of a spiritual father or mother is to lead those who entrust themselves to their guidance from sin to virtue, from mediocrity to holiness. The abyss from which some souls need to be pulled out might be threateningly deep, but even for them, the goal is to reach sanctity, that is, a heroic degree of love, a full conformity with the will of God. God calls all human beings to holiness, but not everyone responds with the same willingness to strive for union with Him—if they respond at all. Many people want only to escape damnation and somehow reach heaven by God's mercy but are not interested in committing themselves to God with all their heart, mind, and strength. The spiritual guide or director serves those who take seriously their step-by-step spiritual journey to God and are searching for the perfection of love, love of God and love of neighbor. Yet everyone is a unique image of God, an inscrutable mystery, and God leads every soul in a unique way that is congenial to his personality and environment. The task of the spiritual guide is twofold, and on both counts impossible to fulfill by mere natural abilities: (1) to understand those one guides and develop a common wavelength to them on the one hand; and (2) to discover to some extent God's plan for them. The two tasks are closely intertwined, for the way to finding God's plan leads through the individual's personal situation and deepest desires. We call this ability to discern God's will for an individual or a community at a given time and situation *diakrisis*, or the *discernment of spirits*.

The guide must search, first of all, for the Achilles' heel of the directee—the sensitive, vulnerable point through which God wants to get his attention. This Achilles' heel could be a great sorrow, a trial, failure, or tragedy, but also an unexpected joy, an overwhelming experience of love, friendship, or success that opens up the soul to the intimations of grace. In many devout people, it is a lingering attachment. We could illustrate this with a children's tale. Burning with love for Jesus, a little boy began praying: "Jesus, I love you very much because You are so good to me. I also would like to show You that I am very grateful to You. I want to give you my best friends, my little sister, my Mom and my Dad, even my ... rubber cat. But sorry, Jesus, forgive me, I want to keep my rubber cat." Most of us cherish a "rubber cat", something or someone we would not give up for anything else in this world. But in the divine-human game Jesus plays with those who want to be His friends, He very often asks precisely for our rubber cat. The spiritual guide's task is to expose the Achilles' heel and help the directee accept his vulnerability so that grace can enter. For instance, the guide may have to explain to a man why Jesus wants him to break up with his girlfriend whom he cannot or does not want to marry, or perhaps why Jesus wants him to quit a dream job that requires long absences which jeopardize his family life. The guide should help the directee discover God's will in his particular situation. Helping someone discover God's will, however, should never be confused with the guide imposing his own will on that person. Thus a spiritual director must be a man or woman of prayer, always seeking the Holy Spirit's vision and counsel above his or her own.

Direction requires careful spiritual discernment, not the indiscriminate application of principles. If the guide lacks the gift of discernment, failure or even disaster may follow in spite of good will on both ends. For instance, an inexperienced director may allow the directee to engage in extreme mortifications that would ruin his physical or mental health and might eventually invite the opposite extreme of laxity or sloth. I heard another example of poor guidance from a misguided directee herself. A priest counseled her to put an immediate and complete end to a deep personal relationship between herself—a married woman—and a married man, a relationship that helped both of them to become better persons and had not diminished their love for their spouses. No unchaste action ever took place or was ever intended by them, as both strove to come closer to God in their prayers and sacramental life. Obviously, the relationship had to be purified and a healthy distance established between them, but the guide should have acknowledged also the positive benefits in the directee's experience and affirmed their expressions of authentic friendship, such as writing letters periodically. God never rejects true love, and in this case, its blanket condemnation by the guide caused confusion and a spiritual crisis.

Another case of poor counseling—and a common one—is to encourage an assiduous striving for devout feelings, an artificial "pumping" into oneself of emotional fervor that will inevitably turn into disillusioned apathy. Emotions of love and delight can in fact support and sweeten our union with God, but without the union of wills, devout feelings are false and deceptive. To be fair, we find the opposite error in some extremely voluntaristic individuals who despise emotions as the Devil's tricks to lead astray the spiritual neophyte, pointing out that strong religious emotions can be triggered simply by electronic stimulation of brain nerves or through drugs such as LSD. While this is indeed scientifically true, God seeks to embrace the whole man—reason, will, and emotions. After a more or less long fight of the will to conform itself to the right judgment of the person's conscience, the

right feelings will normally also appear for the delight and
support of the will. According to Saint Bernard and many
other Fathers, we obtain the desired state of mind on this
earth when uncreated Wisdom, the risen glorified Christ,
occupies our minds and hearts so that our reason, will,
and feelings become united and we delight in the good
and in doing good. For Bernard, such a person is wise:
sapiens, which literally mean "the one who tastes", that
is, who enjoys what is truly good. Hence his definition:
sapiens est cui res sapiunt prout sunt—"The wise man tastes
things as they are." In other words, the wise man appreciates things according to their real value. The body is more
valuable than food, the soul more than the body, and God
more than the soul. Such a man has *diakrisis*, discernment
of good and evil.

Love's Place in Spiritual Direction

Besides discernment, another evident characteristic of the
spiritual guide is *sincere love* for the persons who come to
him for guidance. Such a love must be at once totally
attached and totally detached vis-à-vis the directees. Let us
explore this paradox.

The spiritual director, whether a man or woman, must
be not simply a teacher, counselor, or mentor, but both
father and mother to the directee, attached to him with a
pure love. This is the way Saint Paul, the Desert Fathers,
and monastic authors, in particular Saint Bernard, all understood their role. For instance, Paul tells his foolish Galatians
that he is like a mother in travail until Christ is shaped
and formed in them (Gal 4:19). At the same time, Paul
also boasts that while his faithful may have had a thousand
teachers, they have only one father, Paul, because he begot

them by the word of the Gospel (1 Cor 4:15). Bernard also chastises the bishops of his time because they act as stern rulers rather than gentle mothers toward their people.

Ratzinger points out a fine detail in the Calvary scene of the Gospel of John. At the word of the crucified Jesus, the Beloved Disciple receives Mary *eis ta idia* (Jn 19:27); this means not only into his home, but "into his own", that is, also into his life and into his heart. The apostle John cannot start his apostolic mission until he assimilates Mary's spirit, her tender, loving motherly heart. The Beloved Disciple, then, represents in this scene the entire apostolic college. So all bishops and priests should unite in themselves the strength of a father and the tender heart of a mother.[1]

The spiritual fathers' and mothers' love for their children must also be a discerning love. One spiritual child may need gentle persuasion, while another will listen only to a severe warning. One will be a "light maintenance" directee, the other will need long and detailed instructions. In each case, however, the guide should follow Saint Paul's announcement to his faithful that his heart is not constrained toward them but wide open so that his children may enter (2 Cor 6:11–12). As a confrere once said, "You cannot share Christ with others unless you also share your own heart." If the spiritual children find a welcoming and wide enough place where they feel free "to walk" and open their own heart, a common wavelength is established. They will feel understood and appreciated, and the director will be able to help them.

Saint Joseph gives us a great example of the kind of love we should have for our spiritual children. He loved

---

[1] Cf. Joseph Cardinal Ratzinger and Hans Urs von Balthasar, *Mary: The Church at the Source*, trans. Adrian Walker (San Francisco: Ignatius Press, 2005), pp. 57–58.

Jesus more deeply, watched over Him with greater care, than if Jesus had been his own biological son. That is our model: we nourish and educate our directees for God, as well as anxiously oversee the process of God's image shaped and formed in them. We do not want to keep them for ourselves, but to sensitize them gradually to the guidance of grace so that God can directly guide them more and more, with our help needed only in some extraordinary situations. This is where a loving detachment is essential. Spiritual fathers or mothers who want to possess their children and keep them from growing up spiritually are guilty of "spiritual kidnapping" because, in a real sense, they try to steal them from God. A good litmus test is the way a spiritual director reacts when one of his children chooses to go to another guide. If the original director resents the change, it is a clear sign of selfish love. True love wants the other to flourish and, like John the Baptist, rejoices when it hears that the bride has found the Bridegroom.

HUMILITY IN SPIRITUAL DIRECTION

The more successful a spiritual guide is, the more subtle and the more dangerous the temptation of spiritual pride becomes. We cannot overcome this temptation by humble words. In fact, a hidden pride is more harmful because it might convince the proud person that he has finally overcome it. Self-deprecatory remarks are the most transparent signs of false humility. It is obvious that the self-abasing person wants to be contradicted and praised. If one is congratulated for a talent or good performance, a simple response is what in fact most Americans give: they smile and thank the complimenting person. False humility reveals itself as soon as someone gently agrees with the self-deprecatory remark. Most of the time a suppressed livid rage is expressed by the body language of the person in question. Equally discernible may be the reaction of a proud person when compared unfavorably with someone else. Even if the comparison is made in a very polite and non-threatening way, he may be deeply offended.

An effective way to obtain *the grace of true humility* is to ask God for a sense of reality. We may be saints or geniuses; the fact of the matter is that all we are and all we have comes from God, every natural and supernatural gift. These gifts become truly ours but remain forever God's gift. His act of giving transcends time, and it therefore happens for us always in the present. Our life, natural and supernatural, is like a stream; it "flows into us" in every moment, so it should be responded to in every moment by our actual or habitual thanksgiving. The realistic attitude, then, is to return the credit for all that we are, and all that we have and do, to God, while keeping the joy that His gift stirs in us. He gives so that we might rejoice and "that our joy may be complete". In spite of our efforts, though, a little complacency may stain our joy. Still, when we feel carried away by pride, we can resort to a prayer that God will be eager to fulfill. We should ask Him to heal our pride by allowing some kind of criticism or failure to cut us down to size. In other words, He will allow something to happen that will make us face our limits. If we respond with gratitude to what happens to us, we will come closer to a realistic self-image, and we can better help the directee also to see himself clearly and humbly.

Saint Bernard beautifully illustrates the paradox of our worth before God: If we look at ourselves as separate from God, we are worse than nothing—worse because we are sinners. But if we look at ourselves with the eyes of God,

Whose life and love keep streaming from Him into us, we realize that we are a great treasure in God's eyes:

> As I reflect on my soul, I admit that I find there two seemingly contradictory truths. If I look at its reality, as it is in itself and by itself, I cannot find anything more true about it than that it comes close to nothing....
>
> Yet the Psalmist says: "What is man that you proclaim him great?"
>
> But then how does God proclaim him great who is downright nothing? How can it be nothing to whom God turns his heart? Release your anxiety, brothers: even if we are nothing in our own hearts, in God's heart there may hide something else regarding us. O Father of mercies, O Father of the wretched, why do you turn your heart toward us? Now I know, I have found it: "Where your treasure is, there is your heart." How are we nothing if we are your treasure? All nations are as if nothing before you, but they are not so within you. They are nothing in your just judgment, but not nothing within your loving affection.... In this way you comfort those in your kindness whom you have humbled in your truth, so that man who is rightfully anguished in his own heart may feel great in yours.[2]

Could we find a more beautiful description of the polarities in a Christian's self-esteem? The spiritual guide should appropriate this for himself and teach it to his children.

---

[2] Sermo 5, "in Dedicatione Ecclesiae" (translated by author).

CHAPTER 11

Conclusion

Saint Bernard finished one of his books by writing, "Proinde is sit finis libri sed non finis quaerendi": "This should be the end of the book but not the end of our search."[1] If this handbook keeps alive the hunger of young and old priests to search more deeply the mystery of their own priesthood and find ever better ways of living it, I will be most grateful.

To conclude, I would like to say a few words about our priesthood in heaven—speculation, but with some basis in Scripture. In the strict sense of the word, the ministerial activities of our priesthood will come to an end. There will be no more need for preaching, teaching, or administering the sacraments because God Himself will teach us and lead us for all eternity deeper and deeper into the mystery of His Triune life. Yet I think that in some sense the words of Psalm 110, "You are a priest for ever according to the order of Melchizedek", apply not only to Jesus but also, by participation, to us, who represented Jesus on earth. Just as Jesus, in the act of offering Himself along with his Mystical Body and the entire creation to the Father, remains forever the Lamb once slain Who lives forever, His priests in heaven will participate in this offering. They will also intercede for

[1] *De consideratione*, bk. 5, section 32.

those in purgatory and on earth. The more they are united to Christ, the more compassionately will they pray for those whom they love and who are still suffering on earth and in purgatory.

Here, however, questions arise. How can a person in heaven be perfectly happy in union with the Triune God and still feel compassion for those who suffer? And more importantly, how can God be the perfectly Compassionate One and still be He Who is perfectly happy? Obviously, this is part of God's inscrutable mystery. Yet we may perhaps, by analogies and images, come to see that the mystery is not an irrational sophism but unapproachable light. Human compassion ("suffering with") does not mean simply feeling exactly the same way or sharing exactly the same emotional state as the suffering person. Doing so would instead be commiseration. In the case of commiseration, the sufferer finds solace not in the suffering itself but in sharing the same suffering with others. True compassion is very different. According to Simone Weil, compassion presupposes that the compassionate person is not drowning in the same mud as the sufferer, when the only help he can give is to hold the other's hands while they drown together. Only the person standing on solid ground can be a truly helpful, compassionate companion, because he can reach into the mud and pull out the one drowning. This is the reason why Jesus alone can be perfectly compassionate. His head, so to speak, reaches out to heaven because He is in constant dialogue with His Father, while through His sensitive human nature He can fully empathize with us. More precisely, the same Divine Person Who is one with the Father is also one with us through His human nature. Thus, Jesus can draw us out from the bottomless swamp of our misery, wash us clean, and clothe us with the bright robe of His glorious divine filiality.

We may then assume that in heaven, if we were compassionate priests on earth, we may share (along with all the saved, but having the special responsibility of the priestly character) in Christ's divine-human compassion. We will then be able to embrace—as closely as the measure of grace received allows—the misery of each of our children and help them be lifted up to share in the joy and serenity of Christ.

But before entering heaven, there will be a judgment, and we should prepare for it with both trembling and joy. Trembling, because we are to answer not just for ourselves but also for everyone whose life we somehow affected, by words, deeds, and omissions. Jesus entrusted to us some of His dearest treasures: immortal souls, His brothers and sisters, the children of His Father. And we will have to give an account for each of them. Yet God will also show us how our sincerely repented sins also served our good. We will also see how the grace we have mediated in different ways bore fruit in many souls. We will see the chain effects of both our good and evil deeds. We will also see God "justified" in all that happened to us. What we thought was a cruel joke or indifference on God's part—His allowing this or that tragedy to happen to many good people and allowing evil to multiply—was part of a loving plan of salvation.

Contraception

HISTORY

From her beginnings and up to the present day, the Church has consistently rejected contraception, that is, any direct interference with the fertility of the marital act. The Eastern Orthodox and Protestant Churches, which separated from Rome, were also opposed to contraception until the twentieth century.[1] The Catholic Church has always understood its teaching on contraception as part of natural law, a law that can be derived from the nature and dignity of the marital act. The first departure of non-Catholic Christians from traditional teaching came at a conference of Anglican bishops (Lambeth Conference) in 1930, which permitted contraception, but only for grave reasons. Pius XI immediately reacted with the encyclical *Casti connubii*, rejecting the Anglican position.

The Church's teaching continued unchallenged within her own ranks until the late 1950s. Two major events raised doubts in the minds of the Catholic faithful and several theologians: the invention of the anovulant birth control pill

---

[1] Some of the Orthodox Churches, to my knowledge, still uphold the traditional Christian teaching on this matter along with the Catholic Church. Patriarch Athenagoras of Constantinople was happy about, and in complete agreement with, the encyclical *Humanae vitae* of Paul VI.

and a growing anxiety about what was labeled the "population explosion". The pill, through the suppression of ovulation, seemed to cause only minimal interference in the marital act, and officials concerned about overpopulation stressed the need for limiting the size of families. Pope John XXIII set up a papal commission to study the question, which Pope Paul VI, at the beginning of his pontificate, furthered and expanded. This group of Church leaders, doctors, population experts, and married couples grappled with the issue for many years without establishing a consensus. Finally, two opposing reports, which became known as the Majority and Minority Reports, were submitted to the pope. The Minority Report did not see a possibility for change, viewing the ban on contraception as part of both the natural and divine law, which the Church has no authority to change. The Majority Report, however, held that the only unchangeable natural law foundation of the Church's teaching lay in the vision of procreation as an essential good of marriage and that it was therefore enough for couples to be generous but responsible in transmitting life. The Majority Report concluded that the new circumstances of the modern age warranted a departure from traditional Church teaching, and they recommended contraception be allowed as a means of responsible family planning.

While the commission and Pope Paul deliberated, the majority of the Catholic faithful, and a large number of the clergy, anticipated a change, and many priests had already encouraged couples to "follow their consciences", which practically meant to use contraception. By 1968, when Pope Paul issued his encyclical *Humanae vitae* on marital love and contraception, a majority of Catholics in Western countries had already made the choice for themselves and, if married, had been practicing some form of contraception for years. No wonder, then, that the pope's firm stance on upholding the teaching of the

Church met with resentment and dissent among many faithful and a large number of theologians.

Since then, the situation has changed in many ways. The dangerous side effects of the pill and the IUD (intrauterine device) have been documented, including the pill's potential use as an early abortifacient. Moreover, a newly grown preference for nature's ways—such as breast feeding, natural birth, and organic foods—has diminished the popularity of the pill. Meanwhile, the method of natural family planning (NFP) has been perfected to the point that its observance achieved a success rate comparable to that of the pill without the latter's negative side effects. The sympto-thermal method is still not widely known—no pharmaceutical company has a vested interest in publicizing it—but it is gaining followers not only among Catholics but also among those who prefer NFP for health reasons. In addition, the Marquette method, which makes use of new technology such as fertility monitors and smartphone apps, is quickly gaining popularity.

Overpopulation is no longer a threatening global danger. Population growth is slowing and, according to many experts, will reach a sustainable maximum in the foreseeable future. In fact, the opposite problem faces the West and Japan: an aging and rapidly decreasing population, leading to dangerous worker shortages. A number of experts agree that the most effective way to reach a balanced world population is not to reduce the numbers but to raise the general level of civic, economic, and cultural progress in third-world countries.

The Church's Teaching

The teaching of the Catholic Church can be summarized in three points:

1. Procreation is an essential good of marriage. A Christian couple should be generous and unselfish in giving life to children.

2. Family planning depends on the responsibility of the parents. In planning the size of their family, they will take into account several factors, such as the physical and psychological condition of the mother and financial means. Briefly, the parents are to be generous but reasonable in giving life.

3. Every marital act should remain open to procreation. Any direct interference with the act (contraception) is morally wrong. Natural family planning, however, respects the fertility of the act and therefore is morally acceptable if the goal is right, namely achieving a reasonably sized family. Yet even natural family planning is unacceptable if motivated by selfishness.

The first two are not controverted by Catholic theologians, in spite of a powerful trend in our society to consider children a liability and nuisance rather than a blessing. However, a large number of the Catholic laity and a number of vocal theologians are opposed to the third principle. We can summarize their major arguments in four points: (1) There is no basis in God's revelation, let alone in Scripture, to support the Church's position against contraception. (2) What matters is the general orientation of the couple, not every individual act. If the couple is ready to accept children generously according to their means, they may use contraception in individual instances to achieve this goal. (3) There is no significant difference between using NFP and using contraception. In both cases, the intention and the goal are the same: to avoid or postpone the conception of a new life. (4) Human beings are not slaves to their biological processes. God gave them reason in order to perfect their natural processes, including the natural cycle of female fertility. To the extent that the natural cycle promotes the overall good of one's marriage, there is no need for any intervention. If it does not, one has the right to use contraception to perfect the work of nature.

Those who uphold the Church's teaching can respond to these four arguments in the following way:

1. The Church has the right and duty from God to teach the entire natural moral law, not only the tenets explicitly revealed by God. But that being said, the Church's teaching on contraception is *not* based only on the natural law, but is also a fundamental revealed truth attested to both in Scripture and tradition, which provides a twofold argument against contraception. We have seen that, according to the New Testament, Christian marriage is the effective sign of Christ's love for the Church. The love of Christ means His unrestricted gift of self to each one of us; and His love for the Church is a life-giving love. How can a marital lovemaking that restricts the partners' mutual gift of self by contraceptive devices be a true sign of Christ's unrestricted gift of self? Moreover, how can an act of marital love that has been rendered sterile by a direct interference be the true sign of Christ's life-giving love for the Church?

2. In matters of sexuality, every single act of intercourse is of serious moral significance, and therefore every act influences the general orientation of the person. If a husband is unfaithful to his wife only occasionally, he cannot defend himself by arguing that these were only individual extramarital acts, but "in his general orientation" he has remained faithful to his wife. In

a similar way, every individual act of contraceptive intercourse is of serious moral significance since it vitiates the gift of self of the couple and their creative partnership with God. To put it simply, contraception excludes God the Creator from the marital act.

3. It is not true that there is no real difference between using NFP and contraception. Indeed, the intent and goal may be the same, but the means are different. A good end does not justify any means. In the case of NFP, the avoiding of new life is obtained by abstinence on fertile days, while in contraception, it is obtained by direct interference with the act. The first respects the fertility of the act; the second deprives it of its possible fertility.

4. It is true that mankind has the right to perfect the processes of nature. For instance, in the case of an irregular cycle, the doctor can prescribe medicine for its regularization, and for infertile couples, there are some morally unobjectionable means to obtain fertility. However, contraception does not perfect nature; rather, it drastically interferes with the nature of a free personal act.

To these theoretical considerations, we might add a more practical question: If you are going to use contraception, which form should you use? Sterilization? How could sterilization be compatible with a general openness to life? The pill or the intra-uterine device? The pill and the IUD work either secondarily or primarily as early abortifacients by preventing the implantation of the fertilized ovum into the lining of the uterus. What then remains? There are newer methods in which hormones are delivered by injection, patch, or a device, but these have the same problems as the IUD and pill. There are the barrier methods:

the condom, the diaphragm, and spermicidal foam. Yet as one couple who had used all these protective devices remarked, "It was more like going into battle than making love." This reveals the true nature of contraception, which not only excludes God the Creator from the marital act, but also distorts the mutual gift of the self to one other.

REMARKS ON THE COVER ART

The cover of this book features a photograph of the tabernacle door in the church of Our Lady of Dallas Abbey, the Cistercian monastery where Father Roch Kereszty, O.Cist., lives. It is the work of the artist Billy Hassell and decorated with ancient Christian symbols.

Under the figures, the waves of the sea symbolize the world, as the place of chaos and perils. On both sides, fish are springing out of the water, trying to catch the anchor of hope and the key to the Kingdom—a symbol of faith. In the middle, the Cross of Christ stands as the new tree of life, with the dove of the Holy Spirit hovering above it. The tree is enwrapped by the "true vine", the Church growing out of the tree of life, with abundant fruits—twelve clusters of grapes, symbolizing the twelve tribes of Israel and the twelve apostles, and thus all the redeemed. In the foreground, a mother pelican sits over her nest, feeding her nestlings with her own blood—a symbol of the Eucharist. The two peacocks with their luxurious feathers represent the souls who have reached paradise.

In summary, the images represent the three stages of Christian life: (1) conversion, jumping out of the chaos of the world by means of faith and hope; (2) our life in the nest of the Church, as we are fed by the sacraments that flow out of the heart of Jesus; (3) eternal life in paradise.